Holly Clegg's trim&TERRIFIC™

EATING WELL TO FIGHT

ARTHRITIS

200 easy recipes and practical tips to help
REDUCE INFLAMMATION and **EASE SYMPTOMS**

Library of Congress Control Number: 2013903380

ISBN-13   978-0-9815640-5-0

ISBN-10   0-9815640-5-4

Cover and interior book design by TILT (tiltthis.com)

Edited by Lee Jackson, LDN, RD

Nutritional Analysis: Tammi Hancock, Hancock Nutrition

Other Books by Holly Clegg:

Holly Clegg's trim&TERRIFIC® KITCHEN 101

Holly Clegg's trim&TERRIFIC® Too Hot in the Kitchen

Holly Clegg's trim&TERRIFIC® Gulf Coast Favorites

Holly Clegg trim&TERRIFIC® Freezer Friendly Meals

Holly Clegg trim&TERRIFIC® Diabetic Cooking

Eating Well Through Cancer: Easy Recipes & Recommendations Before & After Treatment

To order books, call **1-800-88HOLLY** or visit **hollyclegg.com** or **thehealthycookingblog.com**

Production and Manufacturing:

Favorite Recipes Press

An imprint of FRP

P.O. Box 305142

Nashville, TN 37230

800-358-0560

On the front cover: Chicken, Red Pepper, Spinach and White Bean Pizza (pg 130)

On the title page: Fabulous Fish Tacos (pg 81), Best Barley Soup (pg 105),
Berry Parfait (pg 200), Great Garden Salad (pg 76)

On the back cover: Southwestern Baked Sweet Potato (pg 120), Lemon Herb Shrimp (pg 26),
Bruschetta Couscous Salad (pg 111)

Eating Well to Fight Arthritis

"This book is dedicated to all of you who live with arthritis.
My hope is that I can make a difference in your life with simple food preparation,
super-satisfying healthy recipes and tips for a more fulfilling well-being."

Why I wrote this book: When I wrote my first trim & terrific cookbook in 1993, I was ahead of my time thinking that there was a correlation with food and our health. Twenty years later, it is apparent that what we eat does affect our long-term health. You might be thinking what is the connection between arthritis and food? After my extensive research and working with the *Arthritis Association of Louisiana*, I believe that what you eat can make a difference and can help ease the symptoms of arthritis. I was surprised by how many people of all ages are affected as well as the many types of arthritis. In this book, I wanted to appeal to anyone that experiences arthritic symptoms, and give them recipes, tools, and tips for a better quality of life. The purpose of this book is to provide practical recipes for a healthy kitchen that will help you eat well to fight arthritis.

My philosophy: My mainstream philosophy, while still health-focused with realistic recipes and ingredients, includes familiar and favorite foods you will want to cook and eat. Affordability, availability, and convenience remain most important as they have always been in my trim&TERRIFIC™ cookbook series. My no 'sacrifice of taste' philosophy is my approach once again in creating delicious, healthy, and easy recipes.

Chapters in the book: Since there are so many different symptoms one can experience fighting this chronic disease, I have divided this cookbook into different chapters for easy reference to fit your individual need. Most importantly, in the beginning of the book, there is a *Healthy Menus* chapter as recipes from different chapters can be combined into complete meals to bring you the ultimate in nutrition. As you flip through the *Anti-Inflammatory* chapters, you will recognize that foods with anti-inflammatory effects are right in line with a healthy, diabetic-friendly diet helping everyone to reduce their risk for long-term chronic disease. The *No Fuss Foods* chapter is dedicated to the easiest recipes to ensure a quick dinner on those more difficult days that you don't feel like cooking. The *Bone Building* chapter focuses on recipes high in calcium and Vitamin D, for those battling Osteoporosis. Some medications have side effects and the *Fight Fatigue*, *Fill Up with Fiber*, and *Tummy Troubles* chapters include recipes to help with these issues. The recipes in the *Spice Up your Life* chapter include spices with anti-inflammatory properties said to help symptoms (and they will just spice up your life). I have friends that have trouble holding utensils when eating so I devoted the *Toss the Fork* chapter for sandwiches and pick-up foods. I admit I have a sweet tooth and that is my reason for the *Because I Have A Sweet Tooth* chapter.

Symbols in the book:

 Vegetarian recipes

 Freezer-friendly recipes that you can make ahead

 Diabetic-Friendly recipes that meet the American Diabetes Association guidelines

 Gluten-free recipes

Each recipe includes the nutritional analysis and the diabetic exchange. The analysis is based on the larger serving size. The nutritional analysis does not include any salt or pepper (since it is listed to taste) or any ingredient with "optional" after it.

Gratitude: Karen Kennedy, President/CEO of the *Arthritis Association of Louisiana* gave me the inspiration to research and better comprehend the correlation with food and arthritis, to be able to create a book to best combat arthritis with food. A portion of the proceeds of this book will be donated to the *Arthritis Association of Louisiana*. Lee Jackson, LDN, RD has been an integral part of this book with her knowledge as a dietitian to ensure we give you the necessary information. For those of you out there, from family to friends, with mild to severe arthritis, I thank you for answering my multitude of questions to give you recipes to fit your needs.

A word from Karen Kennedy

(President/CEO Arthritis Association of Louisiana)

It's so exciting to see a vision become a reality! "Eating Well to Fight Arthritis" developed out of a need for arthritis patients to be able to cook healthy meals and learn tips on preparing meals in ways that are less stressful on their joints. For years I've heard arthritis patients lament that before developing arthritis they loved to cook and prepare meals for their family — but as the disease advanced it was too tiring or painful to do the type of cooking they'd enjoyed before. I also witnessed this in my own life — my mother had rheumatoid arthritis the last ten years of her life. She loved to cook and it was a sad day for her when she realized she had to give up her cast iron pots and pans because they were just too heavy for her RA damaged joints. Even the most devout cooks have a hard time on days when their energy is low or their joints are hurting. The Arthritis Association of Louisiana and Holly Clegg have joined forces to bring a cookbook into the market that can be a source of help and inspiration to arthritis patients. This book is full of great trim&TERRIFIC™ recipes — recipes that are full of the antioxidants that help to reduce inflammation — the trigger of much arthritis pain. There are also great tips on steps you can take to prepare meals more efficiently, conserve energy and lessen the strain on your joints. Regardless of your level of cooking skill, I know you will find many easy to prepare recipes that will very quickly become family favorites!

Karen Kennedy
President/CEO Arthritis Association of Louisiana

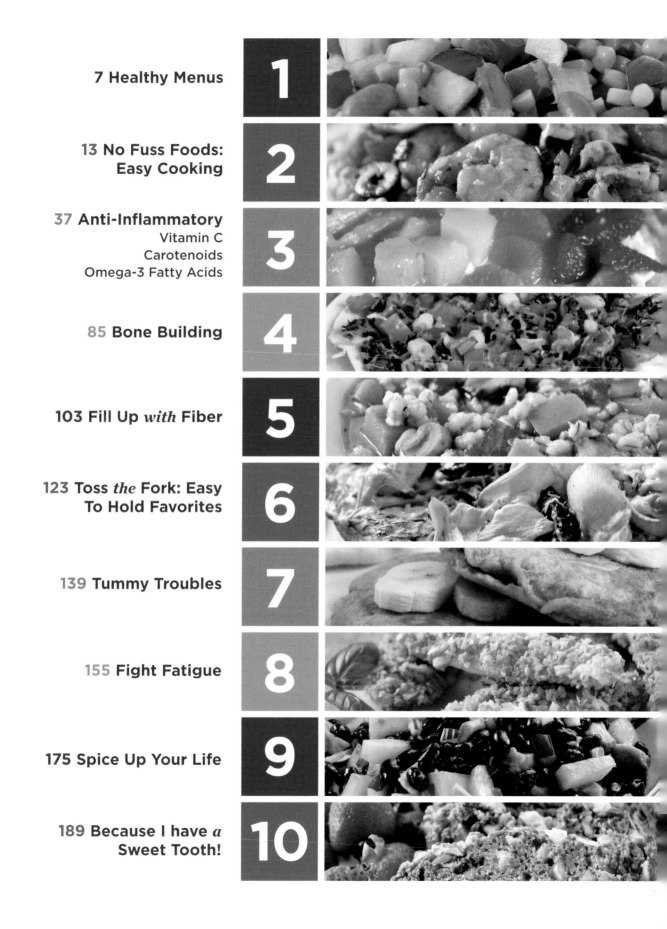

Roasted Seasoned Salmon (pg 82)

1

HEALTHY MENUS

Weekday Menus
Fall Favorites
Summer Sensations
Spring Fling
One-Dish Meals
Vegetarian Entrees

Kale Salad with Fruity Vinaigrette (pg 43)

Mac & Cheese (pg 99)

Blueberry Muffins (pg 56)

Mildly Mexican Breakfast Bake (pg 159)

WEEKDAY MENUS

Chicken & Dumplings - pg 148
Cornbread - pg 101
Kale Salad with Fruity Vinaigrette - pg 43
Peach Crisp - pg 202

Meaty Marinara Sauce - pg 30
Angel-Hair Pasta
Broccoli with Walnuts - pg 100

Caesar Salad (use lettuce stuffing) - pg 134
Stuffed Bell Pepper Bake - pg 50
Oatmeal Nut Cookies - pg 194

Mixed Greens with Apples & Walnuts
with Cranberry Vinaigrette - pg 74
Roasted Seasoned Salmon - pg 82
Spinach & Mushroom Pasta - pg 98
Baked Sweet Potatoes
Fresh Fig Cake - pg 196

Lemon Feta Chicken - pg 164
Lemon Garlic Brussels Sprouts - pg 54
Colorful Pasta Salad - pg 75

Apricot Glazed Roast - pg 31
Mac & Cheese - pg 99
Broccoli with Walnuts - pg 100
Oatmeal Pecan Pie - pg 201

Quick Veggie Soup - pg 105
Open Face Baked Burger - pg 152
No Bake Cookies - pg 203

Baked Chicken Scampi - pg 150
Roasted Honey Dijon Glazed Carrots - pg 69
Wild Rice & Peppers - pg 53

Oven Fried Fish - pg 80
Light & Lemon Angel Hair - pg 152
Brussels Sprouts, Tomato & Feta Salad - pg 110

Diabetic-Friendly
Spicy Glazed Chicken - pg 21
Oven Baked Risotto - pg 34
Broccoli Salad - pg 42
Carrot Cake Bars with Cream Cheese Icing - pg 70

Diabetic-Friendly
Basil Lime Chicken - pg 18
Quick Spanish Rice - pg 35
Bok Choy Salad - pg 90

FALL FAVORITES

Fall Favorites continued on next page

Oven Fried Fish (pg 80)

Shrimp & Peppers with Cheese Grits (pg 52)

Pizza Rice (pg 35)

Baked Chicken Scampi (pg 150)

Glazed Ginger Chicken (pg 184)

Broccoli Soup - pg 41
Stuffed Chicken Caesar Sandwich - pg 134
Yam Chocolate Spice Bars - pg 195

Leftover Christmas Meal
Chicken Cranberry Pecan Salad - pg 47
Chicken Apricot Rice Salad - pg 64
Red Velvet Berry Trifle - pg 199

SUMMER SENSATIONS

Cucumber Gazpacho - pg 87
Salmon Pasta Salad - pg 77
Berry Parfait - pg 200

Fabulous Flank Steak - pg 31
Bruschetta Couscous Salad - pg 111
Tropical Fruit Pizza - pg 57

Pulled Chicken - pg 20
Crunchy Colorful Cole Slaw - pg 63
Southwestern Sweet Potato Salad - pg 61

Spinach Salad with Prosciutto & Melon - pg 108
Crunchy Coconut Chicken - pg 163
Sensational Summer Pasta - pg 65

Chunky Corn Chowder with Kale & Sweet Potato (pg 59)

SPRING FLING

Strawberry & Kiwi Mixed Green Salad - pg 45
Salsa Chicken - pg 17
Quick Spanish Rice - pg 35

Fabulous Fish Tacos - pg 81
Great Garden Salad - pg 76
Banana Chocolate Chip Bread - pg 192

Honey Mustard Salmon - pg 28
Black Bean & Mango Salad - pg 113
Chocolate Zucchini Muffins - pg 193

Watermelon & Tomato Salad - pg 40
Blackened Fish - pg 170
Angel Hair with Edamame - pg 83

Glazed Ginger Chicken - pg 184
Awesome Asian Green Beans - pg 55
Stir-Fry Rice - pg 172

Chicken Cranberry Pecan Salad (pg 47)

Sensational Summer Pasta (pg 65)

ONE-DISH MEALS

Chicken Stew with Roasted Butternut Squash & Quinoa - pg 60

Chicken, Broccoli & Rice Casserole - pg 96

Quick Chicken Rice Casserole - pg 24

One Dish Chicken Orzo - pg 23

Skillet Chicken, Broccoli & Penne - pg 24

Southwestern Beef Casserole with Sweet Potato Topping - pg 117

Stuffed Bell Pepper Bake - pg 50

Roasted Fish (pg 170)

VEGETARIAN ENTREES

Quick Veggie Soup - pg 106

Black Bean Soup - pg 107

Chunky Corn Chowder with Kale & Sweet Potato - pg 59

Best Barley Soup - pg 105

Egg Salad with Extra - pg 160

Great Greek Couscous Salad - pg 180

Bruschetta Couscous Salad - pg 111

Sweet Potato & Black Bean Enchiladas - pg 119

Spinach and Artichoke White Pizza - pg 129

Sensational Summer Pasta - pg 65

Light & Lemon Angel Hair - pg 152

Angel Hair with Edamame - pg 83

Spinach & Mushroom Pasta - pg 98

Southwestern Baked Sweet Potatoes - pg 120

Tex-Mex Rice - pg 162

Savory Breakfast Bread Pudding - pg 142

Strawberry & Kiwi Mixed Green Salad (pg 45)

Stuffed Bell Pepper Bake (pg 50)

Great Greek Couscous Salad (pg 180)

Chicken Tortilla Soup (pg 16)

2

NO FUSS FOODS: EASY COOKING

Arthritis can make it difficult to do everyday tasks, especially preparing and cooking meals in the kitchen. This chapter is designed to simplify food preparation to ensure you get a satisfying, healthy and most importantly delicious meal on the table with the greatest of ease. Ingredients throughout this chapter are modified to be in their most useable form with as little preparation (cutting, chopping, etc.) needed. See the list below for helpful kitchen set up techniques to better guide you to joint ease and pain-free cooking.

KITCHEN SET-UP

- Raise counter top by using an extra height cutting board. Ideal height would be even with the natural bend of your elbows. Too low can cause a person to bend forward causing back pain, or can cause shoulder pain.
- Use a soft anti-slip floor mat to avoid falls.
- If possible, install a pot filler at your stove so that you do not have to walk from the sink to the stove with heavy pots of water.
- If sink filler isn't possible consider using a rolling plant stand to help transfer water to and from sink to pot.
- Use a two step stool to reach cabinets easier.
- Install pull out drawers instead of cabinets so that you can access your pots and pans easier or hang on wall hooks or ceiling pot hanger to eliminate unnecessary bending.
- Arrange your kitchen with accessibility in mind. Ensure that your shelves are set up conveniently with the most used items closest to reach and keep kitchen items near the area they are used.
- Have the bottom front edge of the refrigerator raised slightly so that it closes automatically.

HELPFUL EQUIPMENT AND UTENSILS

- Aluminum pots and pans are much lighter than cast iron.
- Use a pot with two handles rather than one so that you can use both hands to move it around and to support the weight, distributing the weight evenly.
- Opt for lighter ergonomic cooking tools that have easy grips and non-slip handles.
- Use towels around pot/pan handles to make the grip larger and provide an extra barrier to the skin.
- Use electronics such as a food processor, standing mixer, can opener, electronic whisker, and blender when possible to avoid the repetitive motion of stirring, chopping or grating.
- Use a rubber grip to help open jars or if possible an automatic jar opener.
- Use rubber-bottom mixing bowls for stability.

- Specialty rocker knives can add strength and control when cutting and chopping with the motion built in.
- Crock Pots simplify cooking cutting down on pots needed.
- Use storage containers with easy-off lids.
- Keep plastic chip-clips on-hand to use instead of twist-ties for closing bags of food.

POSTURE TECHNIQUES

- Use proper body mechanics. Always work with good posture. Do not lean down to the stove. Use a stool to bring you to the proper height or bend knees or spread legs slightly to bring your body down to the appropriate height.
- Use a wide base by spreading legs in order to prevent stooping in spine.
- Wear supportive shoes.
- When a lot of food prep is necessary, sit at a table instead of standing.
- Take a break from repetitive activity (such as chopping) and give your joints a rest. Avoid all repetitive movements for long periods of times. Take frequent breaks.
- Stretching wrists in all directions will help keep them lose, stretches can be prescribed for each person specific to their ailments.

USE CONVENIENCE FOODS

- Canned, diced vegetables (tomatoes, water chestnuts)
- Jarred, sliced chopped vegetables (jalapeños, olives)
- Look for pre-chopped white, yellow and green onions, and bell peppers in the produce department
- Look for pre-washed and cut cabbage, carrots, cauliflower and broccoli in the produce department.
- Freeze fresh herbs and spices in tablespoons, teaspoons, and half-teaspoon measurements in water. Also freeze tomato paste. Use ice cube trays for perfect 1-ounce measurements.

POTATO SOUP

This simple soup starts with hash browns (no potato peeling) resulting in an effortless smooth and creamy soup. Top with condiments, if desired.

   D

Makes 8 (1-cup) servings

6 cups frozen hash brown potatoes, partially thawed

6 cups low-sodium fat-free vegetable or chicken broth

1 cup pre-chopped onion

1/4 cup all-purpose flour

1 (12-ounce) can evaporated skimmed milk, divided

3/4 cup Greek nonfat plain yogurt

Salt and pepper to taste

Green onion, cheese, turkey bacon, optional toppings

1. In large nonstick pot, combine hash browns, broth, and onion; bring to boil, reduce heat, and cook, covered, 8-10 minutes.

2. In small bowl, whisk together flour with 1/3 cup evaporated milk. Add to potato mixture with remaining milk. Bring to boil, reduce heat, and cook, stirring, 5 minutes or until thickened.

3. Remove from heat and stir in yogurt; don't boil after adding, stirring until well combined. Season to taste. Top with green onions, cheese, and chopped turkey bacon when serving, if desired.

NUTRIENTS

Calories 195

Calories from Fat 0%

Fat 0g

Saturated Fat 0g

Cholesterol 2mg

Sodium 137mg

Carbohydrates 38g

Dietary Fiber 3g

Total Sugars 7g

Protein 10g

Dietary Exchanges: 2 starch, 1/2 fat-free milk

TERRIFIC TIP

I like using Greek yogurt as it is richer and creamier than plain yogurt, while being protein-rich and low in sugar.

Top with green onions, cheese, and chopped turkey bacon when serving, if desired.

Look for pre-chopped onion in the produce section of grocery.

CHICKEN TORTILLA SOUP

A no trouble one-pot soup with pre-cooked chicken, canned goods and seasonings. Top with condiments — avocado and cheese.

Makes 10 (1-cup) servings

1 1/2 pounds boneless skinless chicken breasts, cut into 2-inch slices (or 4 cups cooked chicken breast slices)

1 cup pre-chopped onion

1 teaspoon minced garlic

6 cups low-sodium fat-free chicken broth

1 (10-ounce) can chopped tomatoes and green chilies

1 (14-ounce) can fire-roasted chopped tomatoes

1 (5-ounce) can chopped green chilies

1 teaspoon chili powder

1 teaspoon ground cumin

1 cup frozen corn

1 (15 1/2-ounce) can Great Northern beans, rinsed and drained

1/2 cup chopped green onion

1. In large nonstick pot coated with nonstick cooking spray, sauté chicken over medium-high heat 5 minutes or until lightly browned. Add onion and garlic and continue sautéing until tender, about 3 minutes.

2. Add remaining ingredients except green onion. Bring to boil, reduce heat, and simmer 10-15 minutes. Top with green onion when serving.

NUTRIENTS

Calories 180

Calories from Fat 15%

Fat 3g

Saturated Fat 1g

Cholesterol 48mg

Sodium 475mg

Carbohydrates 15g

Dietary Fiber 4g

Total Sugars 3g

Protein 22g

Dietary Exchanges:
1 starch, 3 lean meat

This warm bowl of soup is a good source of soluble fiber — with beans being fiber rich — helping maintain a healthy weight.

Use electronic appliances such as can opener for extra ease.

Buy minced garlic in a jar.

SALSA CHICKEN

Whip up this quick Mexican chicken dish with salsa and four ingredients. Serve over rice to take advantage of the tasty southwestern sauce.

Makes 6 servings

2 cups salsa

1 cup nonfat sour cream

1 (1-ounce) package low-sodium taco seasoning

1 1/2 pounds boneless, skinless chicken breast tenders

1/2 cup reduced-fat sharp Cheddar cheese

Cilantro or green onion, chopped, optional

1. Preheat oven 350°F. Coat oblong glass baking dish with nonstick cooking spray.
2. In bowl, mix together salsa, sour cream, and taco seasoning.
3. Place chicken into prepared dish. Pour sauce over chicken and bake 45 minutes or until chicken is tender. Sprinkle with cheese and cilantro or green onion, if desired.

NUTRIENTS

Calories 238

Calories from Fat 19%

Fat 5g

Saturated Fat 2g

Cholesterol 85mg

Sodium 776mg

Carbohydrates 15g

Dietary Fiber 0g

Total Sugars 5g

Protein 29g

Dietary Exchanges:
1 other carbohydrate, 3 lean meat

Look for containers of fresh salsa in the produce section of the grocery but salsa in a jar works fine.

Did you know that 1/2 cup of salsa equals one serving of vegetables? All the more reason to dig in!

BASIL LIME CHICKEN

Two key ingredients, lime and basil, liven up chicken for a fresh flavor.

Makes 8 servings

1/4 cup plus 1 tablespoon lime juice

3 tablespoons olive oil, divided

2 tablespoons Dijon mustard

2 tablespoons Worcestershire sauce

1 tablespoon low-sodium soy sauce

2 teaspoons minced garlic, divided

Salt and pepper to taste

2 pounds boneless skinless chicken breast

2 teaspoons dried basil leaves

1. In large resealable plastic bag, combine 1/4 cup lime juice, 1 tablespoon olive oil, mustard, Worcestershire sauce, soy sauce, 1 teaspoon minced garlic, salt and pepper and chicken. Marinate one hour or longer.

2. Grill or broil chicken in oven 5-7 minutes on each side (discard marinade) or until done.

3. Meanwhile, combine remaining 1 tablespoon lime juice, 2 tablespoons olive oil, 1 teaspoon garlic, and basil; mixing well. Slice chicken and pour sauce over.

NUTRIENTS

Calories 171

Calories from Fat 36%

Fat 7g

Saturated Fat 1g

Cholesterol 73mg

Sodium 299mg

Carbohydrates 2g

Dietary Fiber 0g

Total Sugars 1g

Protein 25g

Dietary Exchanges:
3 lean meat

If have fresh basil, this is a great time to use it.

Limes are a good source of vitamin C, with each lime providing almost one-third the recommended daily value. Vitamin C is a natural antioxidant that reduces inflammation.

CURRY CHICKEN

Chicken and four ingredients for a sweet and savory melt in your mouth flavor!

Makes 6 servings

2 tablespoons butter, melted

1/4 cup honey

1/4 cup spicy brown mustard

1/2 teaspoon ground curry powder

1 1/2 pounds skinless, boneless chicken breasts

1. Preheat oven 375°F. Line baking pan with foil and coat with nonstick cooking spray.

2. In bowl, combine all ingredients except chicken. Coat chicken in curry sauce, place chicken on pan and pour remaining sauce over chicken.

3. Bake 40-45 minutes; turning chicken halfway through, cooking until chicken is done.

NUTRIENTS

Calories 216

Calories from Fat 30%

Fat 7g

Saturated Fat 3g

Cholesterol 83mg

Sodium 266mg

Carbohydrates 12g

Dietary Fiber 0g

Total Sugars 12g

Protein 24g

Dietary Exchanges: 1 other carbohydrate, 3 lean meat

NUTRITIONAL **NUGGET**

Curry has ingredients that have been found to have anti-inflammatory properties helping to reduce arthritic pain.

PULLED CHICKEN

Forget barbecue when you can instantly whip up this easy and awesome dish with rotisserie chicken and a few flavorful ingredients.

Makes 4 (3/4-cup) servings

1 cup pre-chopped onion

1/2 teaspoon minced garlic

2 tablespoons cider vinegar

1/2 cup chili sauce

1 tablespoon light brown sugar

1 teaspoon cocoa

1/2 teaspoon ground cumin

1/2 cup low-sodium fat-free chicken broth

2 cups shredded skinless rotisserie chicken breast

1. In nonstick pot coated with nonstick cooking spray, sauté onion until tender. Add remaining ingredients except chicken, stirring. Cook about 7 minutes.

2. Add chicken and continue cooking until well heated.

NUTRIENTS

Calories 170

Calories from Fat 14%

Fat 3g

Saturated Fat 1g

Cholesterol 63mg

Sodium 713mg

Carbohydrates 16g

Dietary Fiber 1g

Total Sugars 11g

Protein 21g

Dietary Exchanges:
1 other carbohydrate, 3 lean meat

TERRIFIC TIP

Chili sauce is found where ketchup is in the grocery. If you want to substitute ketchup for chili sauce, add 1 teaspoon chili powder to ketchup. Serve on sandwiches, sliders or as an entrée.

SPICY GLAZED CHICKEN

In the oven or on the grill, this spicy rub with a honey glaze turns chicken into a quick amazing meal.

Makes 4 (4-ounce) servings

1 teaspoon chili powder

2 teaspoons paprika

2 teaspoons garlic powder

1/2 teaspoon red pepper flakes

Salt and pepper to taste

1 pound boneless skinless chicken breasts

1/3 cup honey

1 tablespoon apple cider vinegar

1. Preheat broiler. Cover baking pan with foil.

2. In small bowl, mix together chili powder, paprika, garlic powder, red pepper flakes and season to taste. Coat chicken with rub mixture and transfer to prepared pan. Broil 5-10 minutes on each side (or grill) or until chicken is done.

3. In small bowl, mix honey and vinegar. Turn chicken again and baste with honey mixture, cooking a few minutes or until honey starts to thicken and forms a glaze (may smoke a little).

NUTRIENTS

Calories 228

Calories from Fat 13%

Fat 3g

Saturated Fat 1g

Cholesterol 73mg

Sodium 146mg

Carbohydrates 26g

Dietary Fiber 1g

Total Sugars 24g

Protein 25g

Dietary Exchanges:
1 1/2 other carbohydrate, 3 lean meat

Don't buy extra vinegar, whatever type you have will work.

OVEN FRIED CRUNCHY CHICKEN

Tasty, crunchy oven fried chicken is always a go-to favorite dinner.

Makes 8 servings

D

NUTRIENTS

Calories 193

Calories from Fat 15%

Fat 3g

Saturated Fat 1g

Cholesterol 73mg

Sodium 546mg

Carbohydrates 14g

Dietary Fiber 0g

Total Sugars 2g

Protein 26g

Dietary Exchanges:
1 starch, 3 lean meat

TERRIFIC TIP

*Be sure to arrange your
kitchen for extra ease
allowing for most used
utensils, pots and pans to
be within reach.*

*Cornflakes may be crushed
in food processor.*

1/2 cup nonfat plain yogurt

1 (1-ounce) packet Ranch style dressing mix

2 pounds boneless skinless chicken cutlets
(or pounded thin)

3 cups corn flakes

3 tablespoons all-purpose flour

1 teaspoon paprika

Salt and pepper to taste

1. In large plastic resealable bag mix together yogurt and Ranch dressing mix. Add chicken, mixing well to cover and refrigerate 2 hours or overnight.

2. Preheat oven 375°F. Line baking pan with foil and coat with nonstick cooking spray.

3. Crush corn flakes into crumbs and mix with flour and paprika; season to taste. Remove chicken and coat with corn flake crumb mixture. Place on prepared pan and refrigerate until ready to bake.

4. Bake 45-50 minutes or until tender and golden brown.

ONE DISH CHICKEN ORZO

Light and delicious, this chicken one-pot meal will perk up any plate. Orzo is a rice-shaped pasta found in the pasta aisle.

 D

Makes 4 servings

4 (4-5-ounce) thin chicken breasts

1 tablespoon all-purpose flour

Pepper to taste

1 tablespoon olive oil

1 (14 1/2-ounce) can low-sodium fat-free chicken broth

2 tablespoons lemon juice

1 teaspoon dried oregano leaves

2 tablespoons sliced Kalamata olives, optional

1 cup orzo

1/3 cup pre-chopped green onions

1. Coat chicken breasts with flour and season with pepper.

2. In large nonstick skillet, heat oil and cook chicken until browned on both sides. Add broth, lemon juice, oregano and olives, if desired. Stir in orzo.

3. Bring to boil, lower heat, cover and cook 20-25 minutes or until chicken is tender and orzo is done (broth absorbed). Stir in green onion and cook one minute.

NUTRIENTS

Calories 332

Calories from Fat 20%

Fat 7g

Saturated Fat 1g

Cholesterol 73mg

Sodium 163mg

Carbohydrates 34g

Dietary Fiber 2g

Total Sugars 2g

Protein 30g

Dietary Exchanges: 2 starch, 3 lean meat

Thin chicken cutlets are available in the grocery.

Look for containers of pre-chopped green onion, and jars of sliced black or Kalamata olives.

SKILLET CHICKEN, BROCCOLI & PENNE

NUTRIENTS

Calories 213

Calories from Fat 19%

Fat 4g

Saturated Fat 1g

Cholesterol 46mg

Sodium 159mg

Carbohydrates 21g

Dietary Fiber 2g

Total Sugars 2g

Protein 20g

Dietary Exchanges:
1 starch, 1 vegetable, 2 lean meat

Broccoli is an anti-inflammatory powerhouse, rich in antioxidants, Vitamin C and carotenoids.

By purchasing a few fresh ingredients - chicken tenders, chopped onion and broccoli florets, this is an easy toss together fabulous recipe.

Makes 10 (1-cup) servings

1 tablespoon olive oil

1 1/2 pounds boneless skinless chicken breast tenders

1 cup pre-chopped onion

1 tablespoon minced garlic

4 cups low-sodium fat-free chicken broth

1/2 cup white wine or chicken broth

8 ounces penne pasta

4 cups broccoli florets

1/3 cup grated Parmesan cheese

Salt and pepper taste

1. In large nonstick skillet, heat olive oil and add chicken cooking 7-10 minutes or until browned and done. Transfer to plate.

2. In same skillet, add onion and garlic cooking until onion is tender. Stir in broth, wine, and pasta. Bring to boil, reduce heat and cook, covered, about 10 minutes. Stir, and add broccoli; continue to cook, covered, 5-7 minutes or until pasta and broccoli are tender.

3. Return chicken to skillet, heating. Stir in Parmesan and season to taste.

QUICK CHICKEN RICE CASSEROLE

Five ingredients for a fast and fabulous family meal.

Makes 8 (1-cup) servings

2 cups chopped skinless rotisserie chicken breasts

2 (4-ounce) cans chopped green chilies

2 cups nonfat sour cream

Salt and pepper to taste

3 cups cooked rice (or brown), divided

1 3/4 cups shredded reduced-fat Mexican blend
cheese, divided

1. Preheat oven 350°F. Coat 2-quart baking dish with nonstick cooking spray.
2. In large bowl, combine chicken, green chilies, sour cream, and season to taste.
3. Spread half of rice in prepared dish. Cover with half sour cream mixture, sprinkle with half the cheese. Repeat layers. Bake 30-40 minutes or until well heated.

NUTRIENTS

Calories 264

Calories from Fat 22%

Fat 6g

Saturated Fat 3g

Cholesterol 57mg

Sodium 468mg

Carbohydrates 29g

Dietary Fiber 1g

Total Sugars 4g

Protein 22g

Dietary Exchanges:
2 starch, 3 lean meat

CHICKEN PARMESAN ONE-DISH

A quick, zesty one-pan version of this classic Italian favorite.

Makes 8 servings

1 tablespoon minced garlic

2 pounds thin boneless, skinless chicken breast cutlets

2 cups "healthy" marinara sauce

1 tablespoon dried basil leaves

1 1/2 cups shredded part-skim mozzarella cheese, divided

1 (5-ounce) package Caesar or garlic croutons

1. Preheat oven 350°F. Coat 3-quart baking dish with nonstick cooking spray.
2. Season chicken with garlic. Cover with marinara and sprinkle with basil.
3. Sprinkle with half the mozzarella, all the croutons and top with remaining mozzarella. Bake 40 minutes or until chicken tender.

NUTRIENTS

Calories 320

Calories from Fat 34%

Fat 12g

Saturated Fat 3g

Cholesterol 84mg

Sodium 678mg

Carbohydrates 18g

Dietary Fiber 2g

Total Sugars 8g

Protein 33g

Dietary Exchanges:
1 starch, 4 lean meat

LEMON HERB SHRIMP

NUTRIENTS

Calories 206

Calories from Fat 65%

Fat 15g

Saturated Fat 2g

Cholesterol 143mg

Sodium 257mg

Carbohydrates 3g

Dietary Fiber 1g

Total Sugars 0g

Protein 16g

Dietary Exchanges:
2 lean meat, 2 fat

*Look in the produce
section of the grocery for
containers of pre-chopped
green onion.*

Serve this scrumptious shrimp and sauce with angel hair pasta and
French bread to enjoy all the sauce.

Makes 6-8 servings

1/2 cup olive oil

2 teaspoons dried oregano leaves

2 teaspoons dried thyme leaves

1/2 cup pre-chopped green onion

1/4 cup lemon juice

Salt and pepper

2 pounds peeled medium shrimp

1. Combine all ingredients except shrimp in resealable plastic
   bag. Add shrimp, tossing to coat. Refrigerate one hour,
   time permitting.

2. Preheat oven 450°F. Place shrimp and marinade on foil
   lined baking pan. Bake 10 minutes (depending on shrimp
   size) or until shrimp are done and marinade bubbling.
   Serve shrimp with sauce.

SHRIMP & ARTICHOKES

My favorite ingredients piled into one simple awesome dish. Serve over couscous, rice or pasta.

Makes 6 (1-cup) servings

1 cup pre-chopped onion

1/2 pound sliced mushrooms

1 teaspoon minced garlic

1 pound peeled medium shrimp

1 cup white wine or chicken broth

1 cup canned diced tomatoes

3 tablespoons sliced Kalamata olives

2 teaspoons dried Italian seasoning

1 (14-ounce) can quartered artichokes, drained

1 cup pre-chopped green onions

Salt and pepper to taste

1. In large nonstick skillet coated with nonstick cooking spray, sauté onion, mushrooms and garlic about 5 minutes. Add shrimp and wine; continue cooking 5-7 minutes or until shrimp is done.

2. Add remaining ingredients except green onion; cooking on low heat another 5 minutes or until liquid is reduced a little. Add green onion and season to taste.

NUTRIENTS

Calories 130

Calories from Fat 15%

Fat 2g

Saturated Fat 0g

Cholesterol 95mg

Sodium 441mg

Carbohydrates 11g

Dietary Fiber 3g

Total Sugars 4g

Protein 13g

Dietary Exchanges:
2 vegetable, 2 lean meat

NUTRITIONAL NUGGET

A lean source of protein, shrimp is also found to be an excellent source of the antioxidant mineral selenium – protecting the body from inflammatory damage to the joints.

HONEY MUSTARD SALMON

Honey mustard glaze with a bit of ginger makes a gourmet-on-the-go salmon.

Makes 6 servings

3 tablespoons light brown sugar

1 tablespoon honey

1/4 cup Dijon mustard

2 tablespoons low-sodium soy sauce

1/2 teaspoon ground ginger

6 (6-ounce) salmon fillets

1 tablespoon olive oil

1. In microwave-safe dish, microwave brown sugar, honey, mustard, and soy sauce until melted together, 30 seconds. Add ginger.

2. Coat salmon with oil, place skin side down in heated nonstick skillet coated with nonstick cooking spray. Cover salmon with glaze, cook 5 minutes or until golden brown and crispy.

3. Turn salmon over, cover opposite side with glaze. Continue cooking 3–5 minutes longer or until salmon is cooked to desired doneness. Add remaining glaze to pan, heat well 1 minute, and serve with salmon.

NUTRIENTS

Calories 295

Calories from Fat 33%

Fat 11g

Saturated Fat 2g

Cholesterol 80mg

Sodium 467mg

Carbohydrates 12g

Dietary Fiber 0g

Total Sugars 11g

Protein 37g

Dietary Exchanges:
1 other carbohydrate, 5 lean meat

NUTRITIONAL NUGGET

Salmon is an excellent source of omega-3 fatty acids, providing a host of nutritional benefits including reduced risk of heart disease and inflammation which helps with joint pain.

BAKED ITALIAN OYSTERS

Reminiscent of a dish from a great New Orleans restaurant, oysters baked in a dynamic Italian breadcrumb mixture offer a rich distinctive taste.

Makes 10–12 servings

2 pints oysters, drained
1/3 cup olive oil
1 teaspoon minced garlic
1/3 cup chopped parsley
1/2 cup pre-chopped green onions
2 cups Italian breadcrumbs
1/3 cup grated Parmesan cheese
1/4 cup lemon juice

1. Preheat oven to 400°F.
2. Place drained oysters in shallow oblong 2-quart baking dish coated with nonstick cooking spray.
3. In bowl, combine remaining ingredients, spread evenly over oysters. Bake 25–30 minutes or until oysters are done and topping is browned.

D

NUTRIENTS
Calories 209
Calories from fat 40%
Fat 9g
Saturated Fat 2g
Cholesterol 52mg
Sodium 524mg
Carbohydrate 20g
Dietary Fiber 2g
Sugars 1g
Protein 10g
Diabetic Exchanges:
1 1/2 starch, 1 lean meat, 1 fat

NUTRITIONAL **NUGGET**

A good source of selenium, oysters help combat arthritis by providing anti-inflammatory benefits.

Look for pre-grated Parmesan cheese in deli or dairy section of grocery.

MEATY MARINARA SAUCE

Doctor up a jar of marinara sauce for a fast and fantastic homemade Italian meal.

Makes about 8 (1-cup) servings

1 1/2 pounds ground sirloin

1 cup pre-chopped onion

1 tablespoon minced garlic

1 (24-ounce) jar "healthy" marinara sauce

2 teaspoons dried basil leaves

2 teaspoons dried oregano leaves

Pinch sugar

Salt and pepper to taste

1. In large nonstick skillet coated with nonstick cooking spray, cook meat, onion and garlic until meat is done, about 7 minutes. Drain excess grease.

2. Add marinara, basil, oregano and sugar. Bring to boil, stirring constantly. Reduce heat, and simmer, uncovered, 20 minutes or time permitting. Season to taste.

NUTRIENTS

Calories 169

Calories from Fat 28%

Fat 5g

Saturated Fat 2g

Cholesterol 47mg

Sodium 301mg

Carbohydrates 11g

Dietary Fiber 3g

Total Sugars 7g

Protein 20g

Dietary Exchanges:
2 vegetable, 2 1/2 lean meat

Meat sauce freezes great so freeze in individual zip-top freezer bags to pull out for meals.

Ensure you are choosing the leanest cuts of meat by looking for those ending in "loin" or "round"

APRICOT GLAZED ROAST

Bold flavors meld together seasoning the roast to perfection.

Makes 12 (3 1/2-ounce cooked meat) servings

4 pound boneless beef sirloin roast, fat trimmed

Pepper to taste

1/3 cup apricot preserves

2 tablespoons Dijon mustard

1 tablespoon Worcestershire sauce

1 tablespoon light brown sugar

1 tablespoon prepared horseradish

1. Preheat oven 350°F.
2. Sprinkle roast with pepper to taste. In small bowl, mix all remaining ingredients. Spread over roast on all sides. Place meat on rack in roasting pan. Cook about 1 1/2 hours or until meat thermometer registers 140° (medium), or 160 degrees (well done), 30 - 45 minutes.

NUTRIENTS

Calories 226

Calories from Fat 24%

Fat 6g

Saturated Fat 2g

Cholesterol 74mg

Sodium 118mg

Carbohydrates 8g

Dietary Fiber 0g

Total Sugars 7g

Protein 32g

Dietary Exchanges: 1/2 other carbohydrate, 4 lean meat

FABULOUS FLANK STEAK

The secret is in the marinade to this awesome flavor.

Makes 9 (4-ounce) servings

2 tablespoons balsamic vinegar

1/4 cup low-sodium soy sauce

1/2 cup Worcestershire sauce

2 tablespoons molasses

1 tablespoon Dijon mustard

1 tablespoon minced garlic

3 pounds flank steak, trimmed of fat.

1. In resealable plastic bag combine all ingredients except meat.
2. Add meat and marinate four hours or time permitted.
3. Discard marinade. Grill over hot fire until cooked rare to medium rare, 4-7 minutes on each side or broil in oven. Serve rare, cut diagonally across grain into thin slices. Let sit 5 minutes before slicing.

NUTRIENTS

Calories 228

Calories from Fat 37%

Fat 9g

Saturated Fat 4g

Cholesterol 86mg

Sodium 416mg

Carbohydrates 4g

Dietary Fiber 0g

Total Sugars 3g

Protein 31g

Dietary Exchanges: 4 lean meat

SWEET & SPICY PORK TENDERLOIN

NUTRIENTS

Calories 138

Calories from Fat 21%

Fat 3g

Saturated Fat 1g

Cholesterol 60mg

Sodium 124mg

Carbohydrates 5g

Dietary Fiber 0g

Total Sugars 5g

Protein 22g

Dietary Exchanges:
1/2 other carbohydrate, 3
lean meat

TERRIFIC TIP

*Tenderloins come two to
a package. If one will be
enough for you to serve,
halve the recipe and freeze
the other tenderloin. Time
permitting, let the meat
marinate in the sauce.*

No time to marinade, this honey mustard mixture gives the meat a
subtle sweet, spicy flavor.

Makes 6-8 servings

2 tablespoons Dijon mustard

1/2 teaspoon minced garlic

1/2 teaspoon dried thyme leaves

1/4 teaspoon pepper

2 tablespoons honey

2 (1-pound) pork tenderloins, trimmed of fat

1. Preheat oven 325°F. Line baking pan with foil and coat with
   nonstick cooking spray.

2. In small bowl, mix together mustard, garlic, thyme, pepper,
   and honey. Coat tenderloins with mixture, and baste
   during cooking.

3. Place tenderloins on prepared pan coated with nonstick
   cooking spray or on rack in shallow roasting pan. Bake
   40-45 minutes, or until meat thermometer inserted into
   thickest portion registers 160°F. Slice and serve.

PORK CHOPS WITH CHUTNEY

Pork chops liven up with this sensational chutney sauce, a touch of sweet and heat.

Makes 4 servings

4 (1 1/4 pounds) bone-in center-cut pork loin chops

Salt and pepper to taste

1 tablespoon all-purpose flour

1/3 cup mango chutney

1 tablespoon Dijon mustard

1 cup low-sodium fat-free chicken broth

1. Season pork chops to taste. In large nonstick skillet coated with nonstick cooking spray, brown pork chops over medium high heat, 4-5 minutes per side. Remove to plate.

2. In same pan, sprinkle with flour, and stir. Add chutney, mustard and gradually add broth. Bring to boil, lower heat, stirring, until slightly thickened.

3. Return pork chops to pan and continue cooking until done and well heated.

 D

NUTRIENTS

Calories 175

Calories from Fat 28%

Fat 5g

Saturated Fat 2g

Cholesterol 59mg

Sodium 179mg

Carbohydrates 12g

Dietary Fiber 0g

Total Sugars 8g

Protein 20g

Dietary Exchanges:
1 other carbohydrate, 3 lean meat

Mango chutney is found in a jar usually with condiments.

OVEN BAKED RISOTTO

No time-consuming stirring needed to whip up this risotto recipe. Arborio rice is the type of rice used to make risotto. Try adding tomatoes, mozzarella and even chicken for a main dish meal.

Makes 10 (1/2 cup) side servings

2 tablespoons butter, melted
2 1/2 cups low-sodium fat-free vegetable or chicken broth
1 cup Arborio rice
1 cup pre-chopped onion
Salt and pepper to taste

1. Preheat oven 400 F°
2. In 13x9x2-inch baking dish, mix together butter, broth, Arborio rice, onion and season to taste. Bake, covered, 35-45 minutes or until absorbed. Remove from oven and fluff rice with fork.

NUTRIENTS

Calories 93
Calories from Fat 24%
Fat 2g
Saturated Fat 1g
Cholesterol 6mg
Sodium 36mg
Carbohydrates 16g
Dietary Fiber 1g
Total Sugars 1g
Protein 2g
Dietary Exchanges:
1 starch

For a delicious option, after risotto is cooked add fresh mozzarella, tomatoes, fresh basil and even chicken.

QUICK SPANISH RICE

Three ingredients create an easy rice side.

Makes 8 (1/2-cup) servings

1 (10-ounce) package yellow saffron rice

1 cup salsa

1/3 cup pre-chopped green onion

1. Prepare rice according to package directions, omitting any oil and salt. Stir in salsa and green onion.

NUTRIENTS

Calories 146

Calories from Fat 0%

Fat 0g

Saturated Fat 0g

Cholesterol 0mg

Sodium 424mg

Carbohydrate 33g

Dietary Fiber 0g

Sugars 1g

Protein 3g

Diabetic Exchanges:
2 Starch

PIZZA RICE

An Italian pizza style rice — add green peppers or veggies of choice.

Makes 6 servings

1 (14 1/2-ounce) can diced tomatoes, with juice

1 teaspoon dried oregano leaves

4 cups cooked brown rice

1 cup shredded part-skim mozzarella cheese

1. In large nonstick pot, heat tomatoes with oregano.

2. Stir in cooked rice and cheese. Cook over low heat until well heated and cheese is melted, about 3-5 minutes.

NUTRIENTS

Calories 199

Calories from Fat 15%

Fat 3g

Saturated Fat 2g

Cholesterol 12mg

Sodium 226mg

Carbohydrate 26g

Dietary Fiber 2g

Sugars

Protein 8g

Diabetic Exchanges:
2 starch, 1 vegetable, 1/2 lean meat

Terrific Tuna Salad (pg 79)

Watermelon & Tomato Salad (pg 40)

Honey Chicken & Broccoli
Stir-Fry (pg 49)

Cashew Chicken (pg 67)

Lemon Garlic Brussels Sprouts (pg 54)

3

ANTI-INFLAMMATORY

The most basic definition of arthritis is inflammation in the joints. Inflammation is the body's immune response to protect and heal us from infection and foreign substances, including bacteria and viruses. Chronic, or prolonged, inflammation results in long-term tissue destruction and may be the underlying basis to hosts of chronic diseases such as some cancers, cardiovascular disease, diabetes, Alzheimer's' disease, and arthritis. Rheumatoid Arthritis, a chronic autoimmune disease, is when the body's immune system responds to normal tissue as if it were foreign and therefore causing damage to it's own body.

WHAT TO EAT TO LOWER INFLAMMATION?

Epidemiology studies show that populations such as the Greeks with a Mediterranean diet high in fruits and vegetables, nuts, healthy oils and fatty fish have less chronic disease including arthritis. Several nutrients may be specifically important in helping to reduce inflammation.

WHAT IS VITAMIN C?

The antioxidant, Vitamin C is a water-soluble vitamin that plays an important role in growth and tissue repair. Essential for collagen formation, Vitamin C plays a role in helping to keep bone, cartilage and connective tissue strong, helping to relieve arthritis inflammation and pain. The USDA recommends 75 milligrams per day of Vitamin C for women and 90 milligrams for men.

FOODS HIGH IN VITAMIN C:

- Bell peppers, red, yellow, and green
- Oranges
- Kale
- Spinach
- Broccoli
- Strawberries
- Pineapple
- Melons
- Fortified cereals

WHAT ARE CAROTENOIDS?

The Carotenoid antioxidants, are naturally occurring pigments that are mostly responsible for the color red, yellow, and orange in fruits and vegetables, but found in some dark green vegetables also. Beta-carotene, a well-known carotenoid is one of 600 carotenoids that are considered "provitamin A" compounds that the body can convert to retinol, an active form of vitamin A. These powerful antioxidants are found to have anti-cancer, anti-oxidant, and immune boosting properties.

FOODS HIGH IN CAROTENOIDS:

- Sweet Potatoes
- Tomatoes
- Carrots
- Brussels Sprouts
- Spinach
- Broccoli

WHAT ARE OMEGA-3 FATTY ACIDS?

Omega-3 fatty acids are essential for the body to work properly and we must get them through diet as they are not made in the body. From reducing the risk of heart disease and stroke, lowering cholesterol, to reducing joint pain from inflammation, research supports a long list of health benefits from eating foods rich in omega-3 fatty acids. Omega-3 supplements are popular, however, the body absorbs and uses the fatty acid much better from food.

FOODS HIGH IN OMEGA-3 FATTY ACIDS:

- Salmon
- Walnuts
- Sardines
- Flax Seeds
- Soybeans
- Shrimp
- Tuna

Although research isn't always conclusive, we do know that overall diets high in anti-inflammatory foods have lower age-related chronic disease incidence. And this makes sense as the same foods that have been touted as healthy – fruits, vegetables, nuts, whole grains, and lean meats – are also thought to have anti-inflammatory effects.

VITAMIN C

Asian Slaw with Ginger Vinaigrette

Stuffed Bell Pepper Bake

Blueberry Muffins

Tropical Fruit Pizza

Shrimp & Peppers with Cheese Grits

Strawberry & Kiwi Mixed Green Salad

FIESTA SALSA

A party-perfect blast of colors with delightful fresh flavors.

Makes 20 (1/4-cup) servings

2 avocados, peeled, pitted, and chopped (2 cups)

1 pint cherry or grape tomatoes, halved

1 cup frozen corn, thawed

1 (4-ounce) can chopped green chilies

1 bunch green onions, chopped

3 tablespoons lime juice

Salt and pepper to taste

1. In large bowl, carefully toss together all ingredients.

NUTRIENTS

Calories 42

Calories from Fat 46%

Fat 2g

Saturated Fat 0g

Cholesterol 0mg

Sodium 26mg

Carbohydrates 5g

Dietary Fiber 2g

Total Sugars 1g

Protein 1g

Dietary Exchanges:
1 vegetable, 1/2 fat

WATERMELON & TOMATO SALAD

An invigorating mixture of cool crisp watermelon, juicy tomatoes, and fresh basil.

Makes 10 (1/2-cup) servings

4 cups scooped out watermelon balls or chunks

1/2 cup chopped red onion

1 pint cherry tomatoes, halved

2 tablespoons fresh chopped basil or 1 tablespoon dried basil leaves

1 tablespoon olive oil

2 tablespoons balsamic vinegar

Salt to taste

1. In bowl, combine watermelon, onion, tomatoes and basil. Whisk together oil and vinegar, toss with salad. Season to taste. Serve immediately (or best day made).

See page 36 for photo

NUTRIENTS

Calories 46

Calories from fat 29%

Fat 2g

Saturated Fat 0g

Cholesterol 0mg

Sodium 6mg

Carbohydrate 8g

Dietary Fiber 1g

Sugars 6g

Protein 1g

Dietary Exchanges:
1/2 fruit, 1/2 fat

BROCCOLI SOUP

Nothing fancy, this velvety soup hits the spot on comfort and flavor.

Makes 6 (1-cup) servings

4 cups fresh broccoli florets (packed)

1/4 cup water

1 onion, chopped

1/2 teaspoon minced garlic

1/4 cup all-purpose flour

2 cups skim milk

2 cups low-sodium fat-free vegetable or chicken broth

1 cup shredded reduced-fat sharp Cheddar cheese

Salt and pepper to taste

Cheese for garnish, optional

1. In microwave-safe dish, microwave broccoli in water, covered, 5-7 minutes, or until tender. Drain and set aside.

2. In large pot coated with nonstick cooking spray, sauté onion over medium heat until tender. Add garlic and flour, stirring one minute. Gradually add milk, stirring to combine. Add broccoli and broth; bring to boil about 5 minutes, or until thickened.

3. In blender or mixer, puree soup until smooth. Return to pot. Add cheese and cook over low heat until cheese is melted and heated. Season to taste. Sprinkle with additional cheese when serving, if desired

NUTRIENTS

Calories 131

Calories from Fat 25%

Fat 4g

Saturated Fat 2g

Cholesterol 12mg

Sodium 200mg

Carbohydrates 15g

Dietary Fiber 2g

Total Sugars 7g

Protein 11g

Dietary Exchanges:
1/2 starch, 1 vegetable,
1 lean meat

Two (10-ounce) packages of frozen chopped broccoli may be used instead of fresh.

BROCCOLI SALAD

G D

NUTRIENTS

Calories 131

Calories from Fat 57%

Fat 9g

Saturated Fat 1g

Cholesterol 8mg

Sodium 111mg

Carbohydrates 10g

Dietary Fiber 2g

Total Sugars 6g

Protein 4g

Dietary Exchanges: 1/2 fruit, 1 vegetable, 2 fat

If making ahead of time, toss with vinaigrette and bacon just before serving.

Omit bacon for vegetarian option.

In a serving of only 5 cherry tomatoes, they provide 15% of your daily recommended intake of vitamin A and 10% of vitamin C.

A memorable and tasty combination with broccoli, edamame, crispy bacon, crunchy almonds, and tart cranberries in a light Dijon vinaigrette.

Makes 8 (3/4-cup) servings

4 cups broccoli florets

1/2 cup edamame

1 cup cherry or grape tomato halves

1/4 cup sliced almonds, toasted

1/3 cup dried cranberries or pomegranates

2 teaspoons Dijon mustard

1 tablespoon red wine vinegar

3 tablespoons olive oil

4 slices turkey or low-sodium bacon, cooked crispy and crumbled

1. In large microwave-safe bowl, combine broccoli and edamame in small amount of water and cook, covered, about 4 minutes or until broccoli is only crisp tender. Drain; transfer to large bowl.

2. Add tomatoes, almonds, and dried cranberries, tossing with broccoli mixture.

3. In small bowl, whisk mustard, vinegar and olive oil. Add bacon and vinaigrette to broccoli and toss well.

KALE SALAD WITH FRUITY VINAIGRETTE

You must give kale a try in this toss together invigorating and dazzling salad with fruit, pecans in an outstanding vinaigrette.

Makes 8 (3/4-cup) servings

8 cups chopped kale, center ribs and stems removed

1 cup shredded red cabbage

1 apple, nectarine or fruit of choice, chopped

1/3 cup chopped pecans, toasted

Fruity Vinaigrette (recipe follows)

1. In large bowl, toss together kale, cabbage, fruit and pecans. Toss with Fruity Vinaigrette (see recipe).

FRUITY VINAIGRETTE

Perfect blend of sweet and savory.

3 tablespoons olive oil

2 tablespoons apple cider vinegar

1/4 cup apricot preserves

2 tablespoons lemon juice

1 teaspoon Dijon mustard

1. In bowl, whisk together all ingredients.

NUTRIENTS

Calories 145

Calories from Fat 52%

Fat 9g

Saturated Fat 1g

Cholesterol 0mg

Sodium 44mg

Carbohydrates 16g

Dietary Fiber 2g

Total Sugars 7g

Protein 3g

Dietary Exchanges: 1/2 fruit, 2 vegetable, 2 fat

Keep kale a part of your regular menu as only 1 cup provides a good source of fiber, 15% of your daily calcium recommended intake, 180% of vitamin A, and 200% of vitamin C!

ASIAN SLAW WITH GINGER VINAIGRETTE

 **D**

Slaw gets an Asian makeover. A quick fix will tantalize your taste buds.

10 (1/2-cup) servings

4 cups prepared shredded coleslaw (try angel hair)

1/2 cup finely chopped or shredded carrots

1 red bell pepper, cored, thinly sliced into 1-inch pieces

1/2 cup shelled edamame

1/2 cup chopped green onion

1/3 cup salted peanuts

Ginger Vinaigrette (recipe follows)

1. In large bowl, combine all ingredients. Toss with Ginger Vinaigrette (see recipe). Let sit at least 10 minutes before serving. Refrigerate.

GINGER VINAIGRETTE

1/4 cup honey

2 tablespoons canola oil

1/4 cup seasoned rice vinegar

1 tablespoon low-sodium soy sauce

1 tablespoon peanut butter

1 tablespoon minced fresh ginger or 1 teaspoon ground ginger

1/2 teaspoon minced garlic

1. In bowl, whisk together all ingredients until well mixed.

NUTRIENTS

Calories 120

Calories from Fat 47%

Fat 7g

Saturated Fat 1g

Cholesterol 0mg

Sodium 152mg

Carbohydrates 13g

Dietary Fiber 2g

Sugar 11g

Protein 3g

Dietary Exchanges:
1 vegetable, 1 other
carbohydrate, 1 1/2 fat

If you can find in your grocery, check out Angel Hair Cole Slaw for its nice delicate crunch of finely shredded cabbage.

STRAWBERRY & KIWI MIXED GREEN SALAD

This stylish salad, light and refreshing, tossed with the sensational Poppy-Sesame Dressing makes quite a statement.

Makes 6 - 8 servings

8 cups mixed greens (Bibb, red leaf, spinach)

1 pint strawberries, sliced

3 kiwis, peeled and sliced

1/3 cup sugar

1 tablespoon poppy seeds

1 tablespoon sesame seeds

1 tablespoon minced onion

1/3 cup cane or raspberry vinegar

1/4 cup balsamic vinegar

2 tablespoons olive oil

1. In large bowl, mix together greens, strawberries and kiwi.

2. In small bowl, combine sugar, poppy seeds, sesame seeds, onion, cane vinegar, balsamic vinegar, and olive oil. Refrigerate until ready to use.

3. When ready to toss salad, gradually add dressing, and serve immediately.

NUTRIENTS

Calories 121

Calories from Fat 34%

Fat 5g

Saturated Fat 1g

Cholesterol 0mg

Sodium 17mg

Carbohydrate 19g

Dietary Fiber 3g

Sugar 15g

Protein 2g

Diabetic Exchanges: 1 fruit, 1 vegetable, 1 fat

NUTRITIONAL
NUGGET

Strawberries are one of the top ranking antioxidant-containing foods and research shows they may also help improve and stabilize blood sugar.

FRUITY QUINOA SALAD

Fruits find a home in quinoa for an amazing and dazzling fruit salad. Add your favorite fruits and toss in nuts, if desired.

Makes 4 (1-cup) servings

1/2 cup quinoa, rinsed and drained well

1 cup water

2/3 cup diced peeled cucumber

1/2 cup chopped red onion

2/3 cup fresh blueberries

2/3 cup cubed mango

1 (11-ounce) can mandarin oranges, drained and reserve 3 tablespoons juice

1 tablespoon canola oil

1 tablespoon lemon juice

Dash cayenne

Salt and pepper to taste

1. In medium pot, combine quinoa and water. Bring to boil, cover, and reduce heat. Simmer 10-15 minutes. Cool completely.
2. In large bowl, combine quinoa, cucumber, onion, blueberries, mango and oranges.
3. In small bowl, whisk oil, reserved 3 tablespoons orange juice, lemon juice, cayenne and season to taste. Toss with salad.

NUTRIENTS

Calories 181

Calories from Fat 24%

Fat 5g

Saturated Fat 0g

Cholesterol 0mg

Sodium 8mg

Carbohydrates 31g

Dietary Fiber 4g

Total Sugars 15g

Protein 4g

Dietary Exchanges: 1 starch, 1 fruit, 1 fat

Quinoa is a grain-like seed that is high in protein, low in fat and also contains iron and fiber – especially important for vegetarians.

CHICKEN CRANBERRY PECAN SALAD

I raided the pantry to liven up leftover chicken and turned it into this outrageously delicious salad.

Makes 2 (about 1-cup) servings

1 cup cooked skinless chicken breast chunks

2 tablespoons coarsely chopped pecans, toasted

1/2 cup chopped green apple

3 tablespoons dried cranberries

2 tablespoons chopped red onion

3 tablespoons Greek nonfat plain yogurt

2 teaspoons light mayonnaise

1 tablespoon apple cider vinegar

1 teaspoon dried thyme leaves

Salt and pepper to taste

1. In large bowl, combine chicken, pecans, apple, cranberries and onion.

2. In small bowl, mix together yogurt, mayonnaise, vinegar, and thyme. Toss with chicken mixture. Season to taste. Refrigerate at least an hour, time permitted.

NUTRIENTS

Calories 252

Calories from Fat 36%

Fat 10g

Saturated Fat 2g

Cholesterol 62mg

Sodium 106mg

Carbohydrates 18g

Dietary Fiber 2g

Total Sugars 12g

Protein 24g

Dietary Exchanges: 1 fruit, 3 lean meat

For ease with chopping, use a food processor.

CHICKEN SALAD WITH CITRUS VINAIGRETTE

NUTRIENTS

Calories 199

Calories from Fat 39%

Fat 9g

Saturated Fat 1g

Cholesterol 47mg

Sodium 222mg

Carbohydrates 14g

Dietary Fiber 2g

Total Sugars 11g

Protein 17g

Dietary Exchanges: 1 fruit,
2 1/2 lean meat

Fast and fabulous, this is a top notch chicken salad.

Makes 8 (1-cup) servings

3 cups cooked, diced skinless chicken breasts (rotisserie)

1 cup red grapes, cut in half

1 (11-ounce) can mandarin oranges, drained

1 bunch green onions, chopped

1/3 cup pecan halves, toasted

1/2 cup chopped celery

2 cups shredded Napa cabbage

Citrus Vinaigrette (recipe follows)

1. In large bowl, combine all ingredients and toss with Citrus Vinaigrette (see recipe).

CITRUS VINAIGRETTE

Makes 3/4 cup

2 teaspoons Dijon mustard

Salt and pepper to taste

2 tablespoons lemon juice

2 tablespoons olive oil

1/3 cup orange juice

1 tablespoon honey

1. In bowl, whisk together all ingredients.

Napa Cabbage is a milder and more delicate alternative to green cabbage. Substitutes: bok choy or green cabbage.

Citrus high in vitamin C protects collagen, a major component of cartilage. Inadequate amounts may increase your risk for some kinds of arthritis.

HONEY CHICKEN & BROCCOLI STIR-FRY

A quick chicken stir-fry that effortlessly perks up chicken and veggies.

Makes about 6 (1-cup) servings

2 cups broccoli florets

1 red bell pepper, cored and thinly sliced

1/2 teaspoon minced garlic

2 egg whites plus 1 tablespoon water, lightly beaten

1/3 cup cornstarch

3 tablespoons olive oil

1 1/2 pounds boneless, skinless, chicken breasts,
   cut in chunks or strips

1 cup edamame

1/4 cup honey

1-2 tablespoons low-sodium soy sauce

Salt and pepper to taste

1. In large nonstick skillet coated with nonstick cooking spray, add broccoli, red pepper and garlic, sauté about 5 minutes. Remove to plate.

2. In two separate shallow bowls, put egg whites with water and cornstarch. In same skillet, heat oil until hot. Dip chicken in egg whites and lightly dredge in cornstarch. Add to skillet and brown 2-3 minutes, turn and continue cooking and stirring until chicken is browned and done, 5-7 minutes.

3. Add reserved vegetables and edamame to skillet with chicken. Add honey and soy sauce, stirring until chicken is thoroughly coated and mixture heated. Season to taste.

NUTRIENTS

Calories 317

Calories from Fat 32%

Fat 11g

Saturated Fat 2g

Cholesterol 73mg

Sodium 229mg

Carbohydrates 24g

Dietary Fiber 3g

Total Sugars 14g

Protein 30g

Dietary Exchanges: 1 vegetable, 1 1/2 other carbohydrate, 3 1/2 lean meat

TERRIFIC TIP

Serve with rice tossed with green onion.

NUTRITIONAL **NUGGET**

Did you know that broccoli is actually a significant source of highly absorbable calcium?

STUFFED BELL PEPPER BAKE

Who has time to stuff peppers? All the components and essence of a stuffed pepper combined in a simple, colorful, delectable dish.

Makes 8 servings

NUTRIENTS

Calories 230

Calories from Fat 27%

Fat 7g

Saturated Fat 3g

Cholesterol 42mg

Sodium 632mg

Carbohydrates 21g

Dietary Fiber 2g

Total Sugars 4g

Protein 20g

Dietary Exchanges: 1 starch, 1 vegetable, 2 1/2 lean meat

Use no-salt tomato sauce to lower sodium.

1 pound ground sirloin

1/2 cup chopped onion

1 1/2 cups chopped red, green and yellow bell peppers

1 teaspoon minced garlic

Salt and pepper to taste

1 (14 1/2-ounce) can chopped fired-roasted tomatoes

1 1/2 cups instant rice, uncooked (try brown rice)

1 tablespoon Worcestershire sauce

1 teaspoon dried basil leaves

1 teaspoon dried oregano leaves

1 1/3 cups shredded reduced-fat sharp Cheddar cheese, divided

1 (15-ounce) can tomato sauce

1. Preheat oven 375°F. Coat 13x9x2-inch baking dish with nonstick cooking spray.

2. In large nonstick skillet, cook meat, onion, peppers and garlic 7-10 minutes or until meat is browned. Drain excess fat; season to taste. Stir in tomatoes, uncooked rice, Worcestershire sauce, basil and oregano.

3. Remove from heat, add 2/3 cup cheese, stirring to combine. Transfer to prepared dish. Spread with tomato sauce.

4. Bake 20-25 minutes, uncovered, or until rice is cooked. Sprinkle with remaining cheese and return to oven 5 minutes or until cheese is melted.

Move over orange juice, 1 cup bell pepper provides 200% of your daily recommendation of vitamin C.

SURPRISE JAMBALAYA

A jambalaya style easy one-dish meal with a cabbage surprise that no one can guess is there.

Makes 12 (1-cup) servings

1/2 pound turkey or chicken sausage, thinly sliced

1 1/2 pounds ground sirloin

1 (16-ounce) package shredded cabbage (coleslaw)

1 green bell pepper, cored and chopped

1 onion, chopped

1 (10-ounce) can chopped tomatoes and green chilies

1 cup uncooked rice

2 cups water

1 bunch green onions, chopped

1. Preheat oven 400°F.
2. In nonstick skillet, cook sausage until done. Remove and drain on paper towel.
3. In large pot, combine all ingredients, except green onion, mixing well. Bake, covered, 1 hour 15 minutes - 1 hour 30 minutes or until rice is done. Remove from oven and add green onion.

NUTRIENTS

Calories 182

Calories from Fat 23%

Fat 5g

Saturated Fat 2g

Cholesterol 47mg

Sodium 288mg

Carbohydrates 18g

Dietary Fiber 2g

Total Sugars 3g

Protein 17g

Dietary Exchanges: 1 starch, 1 vegetable, 2 lean meat

Yes, the ground meat is put in the pot uncooked.

SHRIMP & PEPPERS WITH CHEESE GRITS

Shrimp combined with vibrant peppers in a light flavorsome sauce served over creamy cheesy grits.

NUTRIENTS

Calories 301

Calories from Fat 19%

Fat 6g

Saturated Fat 3g

Cholesterol 158mg

Sodium 496mg

Carbohydrates 32g

Dietary Fiber 2g

Total Sugars 8g

Protein 28g

Dietary Exchanges: 2 starch, 1 vegetable, 3 lean meat

By choosing low-fat dairy products you are actually getting more calcium, since the fat replaces the calcium in whole milk and cheeses.

Makes 6 (3/4-cup) servings

3 assorted bell peppers, (red, green, yellow) seeded and chopped

1 cup chopped Roma tomatoes

1 1/2 pounds peeled medium shrimp

1/2 cup chopped green onion

2 cups skim milk

1 1/2 cups water

1 cup quick grits

1 1/2 cups shredded reduced-fat sharp Cheddar cheese

1 tablespoon Worcestershire sauce

1. In large nonstick skillet coated with nonstick cooking spray, sauté bell peppers, tomatoes, and shrimp, cooking until shrimp are done, about 7 minutes. Add green onion.

2. Meanwhile, in nonstick pot bring milk and water to boil. Stir in grits. Return to boil, reduce heat, cover and cook about 5 minutes or until thickened, stirring occasionally. Stir in cheese and Worcestershire sauce.

3. Serve shrimp over cheese grits.

WILD RICE AND PEPPERS

Jazz up rice with earthy wild rice, mushrooms and colorful peppers.

Makes 8 (3/4-cup) servings

1 (6-ounce) box long-grain and wild rice mix
2 tablespoons olive oil
1 red bell pepper, cored, sliced in long, thin slices
1 green bell pepper, cored, sliced in long, thin slices
1/2 pound sliced mushrooms
1/2 cup cooked white rice
1 bunch green onions, chopped

1. Cook wild rice according to package directions; set aside.
2. In large nonstick skillet, heat oil and sauté red and green peppers, and mushrooms until tender, 5 - 7 minutes. Stir in cooked wild rice, white rice, and green onion.

NUTRIENTS

Calories 163

Calories from Fat 35%

Fat 7g

Saturated Fat 1g

Cholesterol 0mg

Sodium 352mg

Carbohydrate 23g

Dietary Fiber 2g

Sugar 3g

Protein 4g

Diabetic Exchanges: 1.5 starch, 1 fat

The carotenoid-rich bell pepper provides powerful protection helping reduce the risk for certain cancers and boosting the immune system.

LEMON GARLIC BRUSSELS SPROUTS

Fresh unassuming Brussels sprouts pop with flavor and freshness.

Makes 4 servings

1 pound Brussels sprouts

2 tablespoons olive oil

1 teaspoon minced garlic

3 tablespoons lemon juice

Salt and pepper to taste

NUTRIENTS

Calories 112

Calories from Fat 52%

Fat 7g

Saturated Fat 1g

Cholesterol 0mg

Sodium 29mg

Carbohydrates 11g

Dietary Fiber 4g

Total Sugars 3g

Protein 4g

Dietary Exchanges: 2 vegetable, 1 1/2 fat

1. Cut ends off Brussels sprouts and slice in half.
2. In medium nonstick skillet, heat olive oil and when hot, add halved Brussels sprouts, stirring, 6-8 minutes, or until caramelized brown and tender. Add garlic when almost done.
3. When done, reduce heat and add lemon juice; season to taste.

Brussels sprouts' high levels of vitamin C help collagen production and is important for healthy tissues and organs.

AWESOME ASIAN GREEN BEANS

Spunky green beans in a simple stir-fry.

Makes 4 (1/2-cup) servings

1 (16-ounce) package frozen green beans

1 tablespoon sesame oil

1 teaspoon minced garlic

2 teaspoons minced fresh ginger

2 tablespoons water

1 teaspoon cornstarch

1 tablespoon low-sodium soy sauce

2 teaspoons dark or light brown sugar

1. In microwave-safe dish, cook green beans in a little water 5 minutes.

2. In large nonstick skillet, heat sesame oil. Stir garlic and ginger 1 minute. Add green beans, stirring until heated.

3. In small bowl, combine remaining ingredients and add to skillet. Stir until beans are coated and sauce thickens.

NUTRIENTS

Calories 80

Calories from Fat 39%

Fat 3g

Saturated Fat 0g

Cholesterol 0mg

Sodium 228mg

Carbohydrates 11g

Dietary Fiber 3g

Total Sugars 6g

Protein 2g

Dietary Exchanges: 2 vegetable, 1/2 fat

CAULIFLOWER CRISP STIR-FRY

Cauliflower takes a dynamic twist with an easy stir-fry.

Makes 4 (3/4-cup) servings

2 tablespoons olive oil

4 cups cauliflower florets, cut into small pieces

Salt and pepper to taste

2 tablespoons grated Parmesan cheese

1. In large nonstick skillet, heat olive oil and add cauliflower, stirring, 6-8 minutes, or until tender and crispy brown on edges. Season to taste; sprinkle with Parmesan cheese.

NUTRIENTS

Calories 95

Calories from fat 67%

Fat 8g

Saturated Fat 1g

Cholesterol 2mg

Sodium 68mg

Carbohydrate 5g

Dietary Fiber 2g

Protein 3g

Dietary Exchanges: 1 vegetable, 1 1/2 fat

BLUEBERRY MUFFINS

   D

Nothing beats a delicious blueberry muffin—bet you can't eat just one!

Makes 20 muffins

NUTRIENTS

Calories 152

Calories from Fat 27%

Fat 5g

Saturated Fat 1g

Cholesterol 19mg

Sodium 136mg

Carbohydrates 25g

Dietary Fiber 1g

Total Sugars 13g

Protein 3g

Dietary Exchanges:
1 1/2 starch, 1 fat

1 cup light brown sugar

2 eggs

1/3 cup canola oil

1 cup buttermilk

2 teaspoons vanilla extract

1 1/2 cups all-purpose flour

1 cup whole wheat flour

2 1/2 teaspoons baking powder

1 teaspoon baking soda

1 teaspoon ground cinnamon

2 cups blueberries

1. Preheat oven 400°F. Coat muffin pans with nonstick cooking spray or paper liners.

2. In bowl, whisk together brown sugar, eggs, oil, buttermilk and vanilla.

3. In another large bowl, combine both flours, baking powder, baking soda and cinnamon. Add egg mixture, stirring just until mixed. Fold in blueberries.

4. Fill muffin pans about 2/3 full. Bake 17-20 minutes or until tops are golden brown.

If using frozen blueberries, don't defrost. Introduce yourself to whole wheat flour by using a combination of both flours for this recipe.

TROPICAL FRUIT PIZZA

Easy and picture-perfect tropical decadence with seasonal fruit.

Makes 12 servings

1 (16.5-ounce) roll refrigerated sugar cookie dough

1/3 cup sugar

1 (8-ounce) package fat-free cream cheese

1 teaspoon coconut extract

1 1/2 teaspoons grated orange rind

1 cup fat-free frozen whipped topping, thawed

1 1/2 cups sliced strawberries

1 (11-ounce) can mandarin orange segments, drained

1/2 cup canned or fresh pineapple chunks, drained

1/4 cup jarred or fresh mango slices, drained

1/4 cup apricot preserves

1 tablespoon orange liqueur or orange juice

2 tablespoons coconut, toasted, optional

1. Preheat oven 350ºF. Coat 12-14-inch pizza pan with nonstick cooking spray.

2. Press cookie dough into prepared pan. Bake 12 minutes, cool.

3. In mixing bowl, blend together sugar, cream cheese, and coconut extract until mixed. Stir in orange rind and whipped topping, mixing until smooth. Carefully spread cream cheese mixture on top of cooled crust.

4. Arrange strawberry slices around edge of pizza. Next, arrange ring of mandarin orange segments around edge. Then, arrange pineapple chunks in another ring and then mango slices inside to fill center of pizza.

5. In microwave-safe dish, microwave apricot preserves and orange liqueur just until blended, about 30 seconds. Spoon glaze over fruit. Sprinkle with toasted coconut, if desired. Refrigerate until serving.

NUTRIENTS

Calories 270

Calories from Fat 27%

Fat 8g

Saturated Fat 2g

Cholesterol 15mg

Sodium 305mg

Carbohydrates 43g

Dietary Fiber 1g

Total Sugars 25g

Protein 5g

Dietary Exchanges: 3 other carbohydrate, 2 fat

Go ahead and grate more orange rind than you'll need for the recipe — you can grate a whole orange or lemon and freeze the rind until needed. Or, you can purchase dried orange rind in spice section of grocery.

Substitute your favorite fruits.

CAROTENOIDS

Carrot Cake Bars with Cream Cheese Icing

Chicken Stew with Roasted Butternut Squash & Quinoa

Chicken Apricot Salad

Italian Chicken Sausage, Red Pepper & Sweet Potato Sauce

Southwestern Sweet Potato Salad

Roasted Honey Dijon Glazed Carrots

CHUNKY CORN CHOWDER WITH KALE & SWEET POTATO

Corn chowder packed with fabulous flavors and good nutrition; all in one bowl.

Makes 8 (1-cup) servings

2 tablespoons olive oil

1 onion, diced

1 cup chopped celery

1 teaspoon minced garlic

1/4 cup all-purpose flour

2 cups skim milk

2 cups low-sodium fat-free vegetable or chicken broth

1 (16-ounce) package frozen corn

1 large Louisiana yam (sweet potato), peeled and cut into 1/2 inch cubes

Salt and pepper to taste

1 1/2 cups chopped kale

1. In large nonstick pot, heat oil and sauté onion, celery and garlic until tender, 5-7 minutes. Whisk in flour and cook, stirring constantly one minute.

2. Gradually add milk and broth; bring to boil, stirring several minutes or until mixture thickens. Lower heat and add corn and sweet potato, cooking until sweet potato is tender, 6-8 minutes. Season to taste. Before serving stir in kale, cooking several minutes.

NUTRIENTS

Calories 186

Calories from Fat 18%

Fat 4g

Saturated Fat 1g

Cholesterol 1mg

Sodium 91mg

Carbohydrates 34g

Dietary Fiber 4g

Total Sugars 9g

Protein 6g

Dietary Exchanges: 2 starch, 1 vegetable, 1/2 fat

If you want the soup a little thicker, dissolve two teaspoons cornstarch in a little water and add. After refrigerating leftovers, if too thick, add more broth.

CHICKEN STEW WITH ROASTED BUTTERNUT SQUASH & QUINOA

 **D**

NUTRIENTS

Calories 147

Calories from Fat 13%

Fat 2g

Saturated Fat 0g

Cholesterol 38mg

Sodium 276mg

Carbohydrates 17g

Dietary Fiber 3g

Total Sugars 4g

Protein 16g

Dietary Exchanges: 1 starch, 2 lean meat

Keep a lookout for pre-chopped butternut squash.

A one-pot winning recipe full of fantastic hearty flavors.

Makes 10 (1-cup) servings

1 1/2 pounds butternut squash, peeled, seeded and chopped into 1/2-inch pieces (about 3 1/2 cups)

1 onion, chopped

2 teaspoons minced garlic

1 (14-ounce) can chopped fire-roasted tomatoes

6 cups low-sodium fat-free chicken broth

2 teaspoons dried oregano leaves

1/2 cup quinoa

3 cups cooked, chopped skinless chicken breast (Rotisserie chicken)

1/4 cup chopped parsley

1. Preheat oven 400°F. Line baking pan with foil and coat with nonstick cooking spray.

2. Spread squash on prepared pan and roast squash 20-25 minutes or until tender and starting to brown.

3. Meanwhile, in large nonstick pot coated with nonstick cooking spray, sauté onion and garlic about 5 minutes; until tender.

4. Add tomatoes, broth, squash, oregano and quinoa. Bring to boil, lower heat and cover, cooking 15 minutes, or until quinoa turns translucent. Add chicken and parsley, heat a few minutes.

SOUTHWESTERN SWEET POTATO SALAD

A sensational and explosive combination of roasted sweet yams, crunchy corn, black beans in a light jalapeño dressing.

Makes 12 (1/2-cup) servings

6 cups peeled sweet potato (Louisiana yams) chunks (about 2 1/2 pounds)

Salt and pepper to taste

3 tablespoons olive oil, divided

1/2 cup chopped red bell pepper

1/2 cup chopped red onion

2/3 cup frozen corn, thawed

2/3 cup black beans, drained and rinsed

1/4 cup chopped cilantro

3 tablespoons lime juice

1 teaspoon minced garlic

1 tablespoon jarred jalapeño slices

1. Preheat oven 425°F. Line baking pan with foil and coat with nonstick cooking spray.

2. On prepared pan, toss together sweet potatoes, salt and pepper and 1 tablespoon olive oil. Roast about 30 minutes or until potatoes are crisp. Cool.

3. In large bowl, combine sweet potatoes, red bell pepper, red onion, corn, black beans and cilantro.

4. In blender, puree lime juice, garlic, jalapeño and remaining 2 tablespoons oil. Toss with mixture.

NUTRIENTS

Calories 113

Calories from fat 28%

Fat 4g

Saturated Fat 0g

Cholesterol 0mg

Sodium 99mg

Carbohydrate 19g

Dietary Fiber 3g

Sugars 4g

Protein 2g

Dietary Exchanges: 1 1/2 starch, 1/2 fat

Their rich orange color lets you know sweet potatoes are rich in vitamin A and powerful anti-inflammatory antioxidants.

WILD RICE, MANGO & AVOCADO SALAD

 **G D**

Four ingredients come together for an amazing rice salad. Serve room temperature or chilled, a fantastic choice either way.

Makes 6 (3/4-cup) servings

1 (6-ounce) box wild rice
1 cup chopped mango
1 cup chopped avocado
1/4 cup chopped green onion
Mint Vinaigrette (recipe follows)

1. Cook rice according to directions. Cool; transfer to large bowl. Add remaining ingredients and toss with Mint Vinaigrette (see recipe).

MINT VINAIGRETTE

2 tablespoons chopped fresh mint
2 tablespoons white wine vinegar
2 tablespoons lime juice
1 tablespoon olive oil
2 teaspoons sugar
Dash pepper

1. In small bowl, whisk together all ingredients.

NUTRIENTS

Calories 189
Calories from Fat 29%
Fat 6g
Saturated Fat 1g
Cholesterol 0mg
Sodium 7mg
Carbohydrates 30g
Dietary Fiber 4g
Total Sugars 6g
Protein 5g
Dietary Exchanges: 1 1/2 starch, 1/2 fruit, 1 fat

NUTRITIONAL NUGGET

Mangos pack a whopping dose of antioxidant-rich vitamins C and A helping reduce arthritic inflammation.

CRUNCHY COLORFUL COLE SLAW

A vibrant coleslaw bursting with fresh flavors and best of all, one bowl preparation, and one of my favorite slaws.

Makes 12 (1-cup) servings

4 cups cole slaw (in package)

4 cups shredded red cabbage

1 red bell pepper, cored and thinly sliced in 1-inch pieces

1 1/2 cups frozen corn, thawed

1 bunch green onions, chopped

1/4 cup slivered almonds, toasted

2 tablespoons sesame seeds, toasted

1/4 cup balsamic vinegar

1 tablespoon honey

2 tablespoons olive oil

1 teaspoon minced garlic

1. In large bowl, combine cole slaw, red cabbage, red pepper, corn, green onion, almonds, and sesame seeds.

2. In small bowl, whisk together remaining ingredients. Toss dressing with salad, mixing well.

NUTRIENTS

Calories 94

Calories from Fat 41%

Fat 5g

Saturated Fat 1g

Cholesterol 0mg

Sodium 17mg

Carbohydrates 13g

Dietary Fiber 3g

Total Sugars 6g

Protein 2g

Dietary Exchanges: 1 vegetable, 1/2 starch, 1 fat

Not only do red bell peppers add a sweet crunch to your meals, they also provide almost 3 times more vitamin C than an orange!

CHICKEN APRICOT RICE SALAD

 D

Full of vivid colors, flavors and toasty crunchy almonds makes this an unforgettable salad. An especially great meal using leftover chicken, rotisserie, or grilled chicken; even turkey.

Makes 8 (1-cup) servings

2 tablespoons apple cider vinegar

2 tablespoons lime juice

2 tablespoons olive oil

1 tablespoon honey

1/2 teaspoon ground ginger

4 cups cooked wild or brown rice

2 cups chopped boneless skinless cooked chicken breasts or rotisserie chicken

1 cup dried apricots strips (about 6 ounce package)

1/2 cup dried cranberries or mixed dried berries

1 cup chopped green onion

1/3 cup sliced almonds, toasted

1. In small bowl, whisk together vinegar, lime juice, oil, honey and ginger; set aside.

2. In large bowl, combine remaining ingredients except almonds. Combine with dressing and refrigerate. When serving, toss with almonds.

NUTRIENTS

Calories 277

Calories from fat 23%

Fat 7g

Saturated Fat 1g

Cholesterol 30mg

Sodium 111mg

Carbohydrate 39g

Dietary Fiber 4g

Sugars 19g

Protein 16g

Dietary Exchanges: 1 1/2 starch, 1 fruit, 2 lean meat

TERRIFIC TIP

Use kitchen scissors to cut dried fruit into strips. Scissors work great with chicken too.

SENSATIONAL SUMMER PASTA

This is one of those times that fresh is best! A simple recipe with summer ripe juicy tomatoes, fresh basil and mozzarella really rocks!!!

Makes 8 (1-cup) servings

4 cups coarsely chopped ripe tomatoes

1 tablespoon minced garlic

1/2 cup chopped green onion

1/2 cup loosely packed basil leaves, torn or chopped

1/4 pound fresh mozzarella cheese, cubed

4 tablespoons olive oil

Salt and pepper to taste

12 ounces bowtie or curly pasta

1. In large serving bowl, combine tomatoes, garlic, green onion, basil, cheese, and olive oil. Season to taste. Cover, and keep at room temperature at least 2 hours up to 6 hours.

2. When ready to serve, cook pasta according to package directions. Drain and toss with tomato mixture. Serve room temperature or can heat.

NUTRIENTS

Calories 278

Calories from Fat 35%

Fat 11g

Saturated Fat 3g

Cholesterol 12mg

Sodium 19mg

Carbohydrates 36g

Dietary Fiber 2g

Total Sugars 4g

Protein 9g

Dietary Exchanges: 2 starch, 1 vegetable, 2 fat

Serve leftovers (if you have any) as a pasta salad the next day.

Tomatoes are one of the best sources of lycopene, a powerful antioxidant helping reduce the risk for heart disease and some cancers.

ITALIAN CHICKEN, SAUSAGE, RED PEPPER & SWEET POTATO SAUCE

❄ G D

NUTRIENTS

Calories 167

Calories from Fat 25%

Fat 5g

Saturated Fat 1g

Cholesterol 44mg

Sodium 468mg

Carbohydrates 20g

Dietary Fiber 4g

Total Sugars 6g

Protein 12g

Dietary Exchanges:
1 starch, 1 vegetable,
1 1/2 lean meat

NUTRITIONAL NUGGET

Unlike most vitamins in fresh fruits and vegetables, the antioxidant lycopene, actually improves with the cooking process instead of diminishing it.

TERRIFIC TIP

Serve over pasta, couscous or quinoa.

Sweet potatoes add natural sweetness, fire-roasted tomatoes add smoky flavor, and Italian chicken sausage adds heartiness.

Makes 8 (1-cup) servings

4 cups cubed (about 3 medium) Louisiana yams (sweet potatoes), cut in 1/2-inch pieces

16 ounces Italian chicken sausage, crumbled and removed from casing

1 red bell pepper, thinly sliced

1 onion, chopped

1 teaspoon minced garlic

1 (14 1/2-ounce) can chopped fire-roasted tomatoes

1 cup low-sodium fat-free chicken broth

1 1/2 teaspoons dried thyme leaves

1/2 cup chopped green onion

1/4 cup chopped fresh parsley

1/3 cup crumbled goat cheese, optional

1. Preheat oven 400°F. Line baking pan with foil and coat with nonstick cooking spray.

2. Spread sweet potatoes on prepared pan and roast 20-25 minutes or until tender and starts to brown.

3. Meanwhile, in large nonstick skillet, cook sausage until lightly browned. Add red pepper, onion and garlic; continue cooking until sausage is done and vegetables tender.

4. Add tomatoes, broth and thyme, cooking 5 minutes until bubbly. Add green onion, parsley and cooked sweet potatoes, carefully stirring until heated. Sprinkle with goat cheese when serving, if desired.

CASHEW CHICKEN

Tired of your same chicken dish — whip up this marvelous quick stir-fry.

Makes 6 (1-cup) servings

2 tablespoons low-sodium soy sauce

1/3 cup seasoned rice vinegar

1/3 cup dry sherry

2 tablespoons chopped fresh ginger or
   2 teaspoons ground ginger

1 tablespoon minced garlic

1 1/2 pounds boneless skinless chicken
   breast, cut into 1/2-inch pieces

2 teaspoons sesame oil

1 onion, coarsely chopped

1 green or red bell pepper, cored and sliced

2 cups broccoli florets

2 teaspoons cornstarch

Salt and pepper to taste

1/3 cup coarsely chopped cashews

1 bunch green onions, chopped

1. In large resealable plastic bag, combine soy sauce, vinegar, sherry, ginger, and garlic. Add chicken and marinate in refrigerator, time permitted.
2. In large nonstick skillet, heat sesame oil until hot. Remove chicken from marinade (reserving marinade for later use) and add to skillet; stir-fry 3-4 minutes.
3. Add onion and bell pepper; stir-fry 2 minutes. Add broccoli.
4. Mix cornstarch with reserved marinade. Add to skillet and cook until bubbly and vegetables crisp tender. Season to taste and sprinkle with cashews and green onion.

NUTRIENTS

Calories 253

Calories from Fat 29%

Fat 8g

Saturated Fat 2g

Cholesterol 73mg

Sodium 455mg

Carbohydrates 16g

Dietary Fiber 3g

Total Sugars 9g

Protein 27g

Dietary Exchanges: 2 vegetable, 1/2 other carbohydrate, 3 lean meat

There is a reason you were always told to eat your broccoli, it is a good source of fiber, vitamins and even calcium.

PORK & BROCCOLI STIR-FRY

 D

Craving Chinese? A fast and fantastic family-pleaser one-meal dish.

Makes 4 (1-cup) servings

1 1/2 pounds boneless pork tenderloin, sliced in strips

1/4 cup cornstarch

1 tablespoon sesame oil

1 red bell pepper, cored and cut into strips

2 cups broccoli florets

1 teaspoon minced garlic

1 cup low-sodium fat-free chicken broth

1 teaspoon grated fresh ginger or 1/2 teaspoon
   ground ginger

1/4 cup hoisin sauce

1 tablespoon seasoned rice vinegar

2 tablespoons low-sodium soy sauce

1/2 cup grated carrots

1 bunch green onions, chopped

Toasted sesame seeds, optional

NUTRIENTS

Calories 330

Calories from fat 21%

Fat 7g

Saturated Fat 2g

Cholesterol 111mg

Sodium 483mg

Carbohydrate 24g

Dietary Fiber 5g

Sugars 9g

Protein 39g

Dietary Exchanges: 1
starch, 2 vegetable, 4 lean
meat

Serve with rice.

*Did you know rice freezes
so I keep leftover rice in
my freezer to pull out for
occasions like this.*

1. In resealable plastic bag, mix pork strips with cornstarch.

2. In large nonstick skillet coated with nonstick cooking spray, heat oil over medium high heat and stir-fry pork strips 5-7 minutes. Add bell pepper, broccoli, garlic, broth and ginger, scraping bits from bottom of pan.

3. In small bowl, mix together hoisin sauce, vinegar, and soy sauce; add to pork mixture in skillet. Add carrots and continue cooking until pork is tender. Add green onion and sprinkle with sesame seeds, if desired.

ROASTED HONEY DIJON GLAZED CARROTS

Roasting is a no fuss flavorful way to cook vegetables. Toss with honey mustard mixture for a speedy vegetable sensation.

Makes 6 (2/3-cup) servings

1 (16-ounce) package baby carrots
1 tablespoon olive oil
2 tablespoons honey
1 tablespoon Dijon mustard
1/4 teaspoon ground ginger

1. Preheat oven 400°F. Coat baking pan with foil and coat with nonstick cooking spray.
2. On baking pan toss carrots with oil. Roast 20-25 minutes or until carrots are tender.
3. In microwavable cup, microwave honey, mustard, and ginger 20 seconds or until mixed. Toss with roasted carrots.

NUTRIENTS

Calories 73

Calories from Fat 33%

Fat 3g

Saturated Fat 0g

Cholesterol 0mg

Sodium 78mg

Carbohydrates 12g

Dietary Fiber 1g

Total Sugars 10g

Protein 1g

Dietary Exchanges: 1 vegetable, 1/2 other carbohydrate, 1/2 fat

NUTRITIONAL NUGGET

Carrots are so well known for their extremely high antioxidant beta-carotene content they were named after!

CARROT CAKE BARS WITH CREAM CHEESE ICING

   D

One of my favorite cakes; moist and luscious with a divine icing.

Makes 24-30 bars

NUTRIENTS

Calories 145

Calories from Fat 29%

Fat 5g

Saturated Fat 1g

Cholesterol 16mg

Sodium 63mg

Carbohydrates 24g

Dietary Fiber 1g

Total Sugars 18g

Protein 2g

Dietary Exchanges: 1 1/2 other carbohydrate, 1 fat

Use pre-shredded bagged carrots as step saver.

1/4 cup canola oil

1 cup light brown sugar

2 eggs, slightly beaten

1/3 cup orange juice

1 teaspoon vanilla extract

2 cups shredded carrots

1/2 cup chopped pecans or walnuts

1 3/4 cups all-purpose flour

1 teaspoon baking powder

1/2 teaspoon baking soda

1 teaspoon ground cinnamon

1/2 teaspoon ground ginger

Cream Cheese Icing (recipe follows)

1. Preheat oven 350°F. Coat 13x9x2-inch baking pan with nonstick cooking spray.

2. In large bowl, whisk together oil, brown sugar, eggs, orange juice, and vanilla. Stir in carrots and pecans.

3. In another bowl combine flour, baking powder, baking soda, cinnamon, and ginger. Add to carrot mixture; stirring just until combined. Spread batter into prepared pan. Bake 17-20 minutes or until toothpick inserted in center comes out clean. Cool and ice with Cream Cheese Icing (see recipe).

CREAM CHEESE ICING

4 ounces reduced-fat cream cheese

1 tablespoon butter

2 1/2 cups confectioners' sugar

1 tablespoon orange juice

1. In mixing bowl, beat together all ingredients until creamy.

See page 58 for photo

OMEGA-3 FATTY ACIDS

Spiced Walnuts

Great Garden Salad

Fabulous Fish Tacos

Guacamame

Roasted Seasoned Salmon

Salmon Bisque

GUACAMAME

Avocado and edamame makes this delicious dip. Serve with veggies or chips.

Makes 10 (1/4-cup) servings

1 large avocado, (about 2/3 cup mashed)

1 1/2 cups shelled edamame, thawed

2 tablespoons lime juice

1/2 teaspoon minced garlic

1/2 cup salsa

3 tablespoons Greek nonfat plain yogurt

Salt and pepper to taste

1. In food processor, mix all ingredients, until smooth.

NUTRIENTS

Calories 62

Calories from Fat 47%

Fat 3g

Saturated Fat 0g

Cholesterol 0mg

Sodium 50mg

Carbohydrates 5g

Dietary Fiber 2g

Total Sugars 2g

Protein 4g

Dietary Exchanges: 1 vegetable, 1/2 fat

SPICED WALNUTS

Wonderful walnuts with a touch of spice, heat and sweet.

Makes 8 (1/4-cup) servings

2 cups walnut halves

1 tablespoon sugar

1/4 teaspoon salt

1/2 teaspoon garlic powder

1/2 teaspoon ground cumin

1/4 teaspoon ground cinnamon

1/4 teaspoon cayenne

1 tablespoon canola oil

1. Preheat oven 375°F.

2. Spread walnuts on baking pan and bake about 5-7 minutes or until golden. In small bowl, combine sugar, salt, garlic powder, cumin, cinnamon, and cayenne.

3. In nonstick skillet, heat oil over medium heat. Add nuts and stir to coat with oil. Add seasoning mix, stirring until nuts coated. Remove to paper towel to cool.

NUTRIENTS

Calories 99

Calories from fat 46%

Fat 5g

Saturated Fat 1g

Cholesterol 4mg

Sodium 210mg

Carbohydrate 8g

Dietary Fiber 3g

Sugars 4g

Protein 6g

Diabetic Exchanges: 1/2 starch, 1 lean meat, 1/2 fat

SALMON BISQUE

A mouth-watering easy and elegant salmon lover's soup. Great recipe to use leftover salmon.

Makes 8 (1-cup) servings

2 tablespoons butter

1/4 cup finely chopped onion

1/3 cup all-purpose flour

1 cup low-sodium fat-free chicken broth

1 cup fat-free half-and-half

1/2 cup skim milk

1 tablespoon tomato paste

1/2 cup white wine

2 cups cooked, skin removed, flaked salmon fillet (pan sauté, broil, grill or poach)

1 teaspoon dried dill weed leaves

Salt and white pepper to taste

1. In large nonstick pot, melt butter and sauté onion about 3 minutes, cooking until tender.
2. Gradually blend in flour, stirring 1 minute. Add broth, half-and-half, milk and tomato paste, stirring constantly. Bring to boil, reduce heat, stirring until mixture starts to thicken. Add wine and continue cooking until thickened.
3. Add flaked salmon, dill weed, and season to taste.

NUTRIENTS

Calories 135

Calories from Fat 32%

Fat 5g

Saturated Fat 2g

Cholesterol 27mg

Sodium 109mg

Carbohydrates 10g

Dietary Fiber 0g

Total Sugars 3g

Protein 12g

Dietary Exchanges: 1/2 starch, 1 1/2 lean meat

Not only is salmon rich in omega-3 fatty acids, it is also an excellent source of bone maintaining vitamin D and selenium — helping prevent oxidative stress and inflammation.

Don't let the word bisque intimidate you, as bisque is a thick, creamy soup.

MIXED GREENS WITH APPLES & WALNUTS WITH CRANBERRY VINAIGRETTE

G D

Tart apples, sweet cranberries and toasted walnuts with a lightly sweetened vinaigrette makes this a special salad with lots of flair.

Makes 6 servings

1 cup sliced green apples

1/2 cup thinly sliced red onion

1/3 cup dried cranberries

1/3 cup chopped walnuts, toasted

6 cups mixed greens

1/4 cup crumbled reduced-fat feta cheese

Cranberry Vinaigrette, (recipe follows)

1. In bowl, combine apples, onion, cranberries, walnuts and mixed greens. Toss with feta and Cranberry Vinaigrette (see recipe).

NUTRIENTS

Calories 149

Calories from fat 43%

Fat 7g

Saturated Fat 1g

Cholesterol 3mg

Sodium 118mg

Carbohydrate 19g

Dietary Fiber 2g

Sugars 15g

Protein 4g

Dietary Exchanges: 1 fruit, 1 vegetable, 1 1/2 fat

TERRIFIC TIP

Use a soft anti-slip floor mat in the kitchen to avoid falls.

CRANBERRY VINAIGRETTE

Use this fantastic vinaigrette on your favorite salad.

1 tablespoon honey

2 tablespoons cranberry cocktail juice

1/3 cup balsamic vinegar

1 teaspoon Dijon mustard

1 tablespoon olive oil

Salt and pepper to taste

2 tablespoons nonfat sour cream

1. In small bowl, whisk together honey, cranberry juice, vinegar, mustard, oil, and season to taste. Whisk in sour cream.

COLORFUL PASTA SALAD

This eye-catching vegetarian salad is packed with mouth-watering fresh flavors.

 D

Makes 8 (1/2-cup) servings

8 ounces tri-colored spiral pasta

1 1/2 cups broccoli florets

1/2 cup shredded carrots

1/2 cup chopped green onion

1/4 cup shelled edamame, cooked according to package directions

2 tablespoons sliced Kalamata olives

1/4 cup chopped walnuts, toasted

1/4 cup dried cranberries

1/4 cup Light Raspberry and Walnut Dressing or light dressing of choice

1. Cook pasta according to package directions, drain.
2. In large bowl, combine all ingredients with cooked pasta except dressing. Toss with dressing.

NUTRIENTS

Calories 181

Calories from fat 24%

Fat 5g

Saturated Fat 0g

Cholesterol 0mg

Sodium 123mg

Carbohydrate 29g

Dietary Fiber 2g

Sugars 6g

Protein 5g

Diabetic Exchanges: 2 starch, 1 fat

For extra ease, take short-cuts with pre-chopped broccoli florets, pre-shredded carrots, and jarred sliced olives.

Toss in grilled shrimp or leftover chicken, for main dish salad.

GREAT GARDEN SALAD

Color equals nutrition and this salad is overflowing with color, flavor, and garden fresh favorites.

Makes 6 (2/3-cup) servings

1 1/2 cups fresh or frozen corn

1 cup chopped tomatoes

1 cup chopped peeled cucumber

1/3 cup shelled edamame, cooked according to directions and drained

1/2 cup chopped red onion

1/3 cup chopped avocado

2 tablespoons lime juice

1 tablespoon olive oil

Salt and pepper to taste

1. In bowl, combine corn, tomatoes, cucumber, edamame, red onion, and avocado.

2. In small bowl, whisk together lime juice and oil. Toss with corn mixture and season to taste.

NUTRIENTS

Calories 92

Calories from fat 42%

Fat 4g

Saturated Fat 1g

Cholesterol 0mg

Sodium 9mg

Carbohydrate 12g

Dietary Fiber 3g

Sugars 3g

Protein 3g

Diabetic Exchanges: 1/2 starch, 1 vegetable, 1/2 fat

SALMON PASTA SALAD

Fresh salmon is worth the extra effort, for this entree salad, but to save time, you can substitute a can of red salmon or tuna.

Makes 6 (1 1/3-cup) servings

1 pound fresh salmon fillet

Salt and pepper to taste

1 (8-ounce) package rotini (spiral) pasta

1/3 cup light mayonnaise

1/2 cup nonfat plain yogurt

1/2 teaspoon sugar

2 teaspoons dried dill weed leaves

1/2 teaspoon white pepper

1 cup diced celery

1/2 cup chopped red onion

1 (14-ounce) can artichoke hearts, drained and quartered

1. Preheat oven 325°F. Line baking pan with foil and coat with nonstick cooking spray.

2. Season salmon. Bake 15 minutes, or until salmon is done and flakes easily. Cool, remove skin, and flake into chunks.

3. Cook pasta according to package directions. Drain, rinse, set aside.

4. In small bowl, mix mayonnaise, yogurt, sugar, dill weed, and pepper; set aside. In large bowl, mix together celery, red onion, artichokes, pasta, and mayonnaise mixture. Carefully add flaked salmon, tossing gently. Refrigerate.

D

NUTRIENTS

Calories 307

Calories from Fat 21%

Fat 7g

Saturated Fat 1g

Cholesterol 40mg

Sodium 327mg

Carbohydrates 36g

Dietary Fiber 2g

Total Sugars 5g

Protein 23g

Dietary Exchanges: 2 starch, 1 vegetable, 2 lean meat

TERRIFIC TIP

Fresh herbs can be substituted for dried herbs at a ratio of 3:1. In other words, 1 tablespoon of fresh herbs = 1 teaspoon dried.

Salmon may be pan-seared instead of baking.

SMOKED SALMON EGG SALAD

NUTRIENTS

Calories 105

Calories from Fat 61%

Fat 7g

Saturated Fat 2g

Cholesterol 126mg

Sodium 358mg

Carbohydrates 2g

Dietary Fiber 0g

Total Sugars 1g

Protein 8g

Dietary Exchanges: 1 lean meat, 1 fat

NUTRITIONAL NUGGET

Fatty fish contains vitamin D, which helps to prevent swelling and soreness.

Turn an ordinary egg salad into a gourmet delight featuring smoked salmon with all the condiments.

Makes 6 (1/2-cup) servings

4 hard boiled eggs, chopped

4 hard boiled eggs, whites only, chopped

1/3 cup finely chopped red onion

2 tablespoons capers, drained

1 tablespoon finely chopped fresh dill weed or 1 teaspoon dried dill weed

1 tablespoon lemon juice

2 ounces smoked salmon, diced

1 1/2 tablespoons olive oil

Pepper

1. In large bowl, combine chopped eggs, egg whites, red onion, capers, dill, lemon juice and salmon. Drizzle with oil and carefully combine. Add pepper to taste.

TERRIFIC TUNA SALAD

Open a few cans and you have a fantastic and unique tuna salad.

Makes 6 (1-cup) servings

1 (12-ounce) can albacore white tuna, packed in water, drained

1 (11-ounce) can mandarin oranges, drained

1/4 pound fresh mushrooms, sliced

1 (14-ounce) can quartered artichoke hearts, drained

1 (8-ounce) can sliced water chestnuts, drained

1/2 cup chopped green onion

Dressing, (recipe follows)

1. Carefully combine all ingredients in large bowl. Toss with dressing (see recipe).

DRESSING

1/3 cup nonfat plain yogurt

2 tablespoons light mayonnaise

1 tablespoon lemon juice

1 teaspoon sugar

1. Combine all ingredients together and fold into tuna mixture.

NUTRIENTS

Calories 161

Calories from Fat 17%

Fat 3g

Saturated Fat 1g

Cholesterol 26mg

Sodium 396mg

Carbohydrate 18g

Dietary Fiber 3g

Protein 16g

Sugars 11g

Diabetic Exchanges: 1 fruit, 1 vegetable, 2 lean meat

Serve over mixed greens, spinach, or on sandwich.

OVEN FRIED FISH

This is as close to crunchy fried fish as you can get; and the secret is to start with a heated pan.

Makes 6 servings

2 tablespoons olive oil

2/3 cup buttermilk

Hot sauce to taste

2 teaspoons Dijon mustard

1 teaspoon minced garlic

Salt and pepper to taste

1 1/2 pounds fish fillets

2/3 cup all-purpose flour

2/3 cup yellow cornmeal

1. Preheat oven 475°F. Coat baking pan with oil and heat in oven.

2. In zip-top plastic bag, combine buttermilk, hot sauce, mustard and garlic. Season fish to taste and add to buttermilk mixture. Let sit 15 minutes.

3. In shallow bowl or plate, mix flour and cornmeal together. Remove fish from buttermilk, letting excess drip off, and dredge on both sides with cornmeal mixture. Transfer to hot baking pan.

4. Bake 6 minutes, then carefully turn fish and continue cooking 5 minutes more, or until cooked through and golden.

D

NUTRIENTS

Calories 173

Calories from Fat 24%

Fat 4g

Saturated Fat 1g

Cholesterol 44mg

Sodium 93mg

Carbohydrates 13g

Dietary Fiber 1g

Total Sugars 1g

Protein 20g

Dietary Exchanges: 1 starch, 3 lean meat

Fish options high in omega-3 include mackerel and rainbow trout.

Using a heated oiled pan gives the fish a more crispy coating.

FABULOUS FISH TACOS

Taco-seasoned fish topped with mild creamy coleslaw and tomatoes served in a corn tortilla is the best of southwestern and seafood.

Makes 8 servings

1 1/2 pounds fish fillets

1 (1.25-ounce) package low-sodium taco seasoning mix

2 tablespoons lime juice

2 cups cole slaw (shredded cabbage)

1/3 cup nonfat sour cream

1 tablespoon light mayonnaise

1 bunch green onion, chopped

3 tablespoons chopped green chilies

Salt and pepper to taste

8 (6-inch) corn tortillas

1. In bowl or plastic bag, coat fish with taco seasoning and lime juice.
2. In large nonstick skillet coated with nonstick cooking spray, sauté fish over medium heat 5–7 minutes, until flaky and done.
3. In bowl, combine coleslaw, sour cream, mayonnaise, green onion, green chilies, season to taste; set aside.
4. Warm tortillas according to package directions or heat in microwave 30 seconds. Fill each tortilla with fish and coleslaw mixture. Repeat with remaining tortillas.

D

NUTRIENTS

Calories 144

Calories from fat 9%

Fat 2g

Saturated Fat 0g

Cholesterol 35mg

Sodium 344mg

Carbohydrate 15g

Dietary Fiber 3g

Sugars 3g

Protein 15g

Diabetic Exchanges: 1 starch, 2 lean meat

TERRIFIC TIP

Check produce area in grocery for bag of shredded cabbage or coleslaw for this recipe.

Serve with avocados, if desired.

ROASTED SEASONED SALMON

NUTRIENTS
Calories 257

Calories from Fat 29%

Fat 8g

Saturated Fat 1g

Cholesterol 80mg

Sodium 177mg

Carbohydrates 8g

Dietary Fiber 1g

Total Sugars 7g

Protein 36g

Dietary Exchanges: 1/2 other carbohydrate, 5 lean meat

NUTRITIONAL NUGGET

At least two servings of fish (fatty fish preferred) per week is the recommended intake by the American Heart Association.

Simple seasonings perk up salmon with a sweet and spicy rub. Easy to make and oh-so enjoyable to eat.

Makes 4 servings

2 tablespoons light brown sugar

4 teaspoons chili powder

1 teaspoon ground cumin

1/4 teaspoon ground cinnamon

Salt and pepper to taste

4 (6-ounce) salmon fillets

1. Preheat oven 400°F. Coat 11x7x2-inch baking dish coated with nonstick cooking spray.

2. In small bowl, mix together brown sugar, chili powder, cumin, cinnamon and season to taste. Rub over salmon and place in prepared dish.

3. Bake 12 - 15 minutes or until fish flakes easily when tested with fork.

ANGEL HAIR WITH EDAMAME

This simple yet delightful dish with edamame, garlic and parsley ranks high on the pasta charts.

Makes 4 servings

8 ounces angel hair (whole wheat pasta)

1 cup shelled edamame

2 tablespoons olive oil

1 teaspoon minced garlic

3 tablespoons minced parsley

Salt and pepper to taste

1. Cook pasta according to package directions. Drain and set aside.

2. Cook edamame in microwave according to package directions, set aside.

3. In skillet (or use same pot pasta cooked in), heat oil and sauté garlic and parsley about one minute. Add pasta and edamame, toss, and season to taste.

NUTRIENTS

Calories 322

Calories from Fat 27%

Fat 9g

Saturated Fat 1g

Cholesterol 0mg

Sodium 8mg

Carbohydrates 46g

Dietary Fiber 3g

Total Sugars 3g

Protein 12g

Dietary Exchanges: 3 starch, 1/2 lean meat, 1 fat

NUTRITIONAL NUGGET

Soybeans, or edamame, are a good source of fiber, 1 cup cooked providing over 40% of your daily recommended intake.

Strawberry Fruit Dip (pg 88)

4

BONE BUILDING

Osteoporosis is the most common bone disease, causing thinning of bone tissue and bone density loss. Healthy bone regularly breaks down bone tissue while cells use calcium, vitamin D and other nutrients, largely from the diet, to build up new bone. Problems occur when the normal bone tissue breakdown is not replaced with bone-building nutrients, leaving bones weak. Poor nutrition and age are risk factors for osteoporosis. This is why getting the recommended amount of these important nutrients are vital for healthy bone.

WHAT IS CALCIUM?

Calcium is the most abundant mineral in the body, and is required for many important metabolic, vascular and muscular functions. However, only 1% is needed for these highly regulated mineral functions, as 99% of the calcium in the body is stored in the bones making it the main nutrient for bone health.

FOODS HIGH IN CALCIUM:

- Dairy products — Milk, cheese, yogurt, pudding
- Dark leafy greens — Kale, broccoli, Chinese cabbage, bok choy
- Almonds
- Fortified cereal
- Tofu

WHAT IS VITAMIN D?

Vitamin D plays a major role in strong bone health by maintaining calcium and phosphorus levels in the blood. The fat-soluble vitamin D is vital for the absorption of calcium helping to maintain bone density, and decrease risk of fracture and osteoporosis. Although few foods have the vitamin naturally present, milk, orange juice and cereal are often fortified. Known as the "Sunshine Vitamin," sun exposure allows the body to produce vitamin D when the ultraviolet light hits the skin. Most people meet their recommended intake with only 10-30 minutes of sunlight two to three times per week.

FOODS HIGH IN VITAMIN D:

- Fish — Salmon, Tuna, Mackerel
- Milk, fortified
- Orange juice, fortified
- Egg yolks
- Ready-to-eat cereal
- Cod Liver oil

AVOID NEGATIVE BONE-BUILDING FACTORS:

ALCOHOL: New studies have found that moderate alcohol consumption may have a positive effect on bone health, causing decreased bone turnover – reducing the risk of osteoporotic fractures. However, chronic heavy alcohol intake dramatically increases the risk for osteoporosis and reduced bone health.

SMOKING: A definite risk factor for osteoporosis, cigarette smoking, and tobacco use result in decreased bone density. What isn't clear is if it is the actual tobacco that causes the bone density to diminish or if it is the circumstances that often surround smoking, i.e. smokers tend to be thinner, eat less nutritive foods, drink more alcohol, and exercise less.

SODA: There is a link between soda consumption and osteoporosis, partly due to the fact that the more soda one drinks, often the less calcium and vitamin d fortified milk and orange juice is consumed. Besides replacing healthier alternatives with soda, research also suggests that cola-based beverages have phosphorus that when ingested at a disproportionate ratio to calcium leads to loss of bone density. Caffeine may also play a role in calcium mal-absorption.

WEIGHT-BEARING EXERCISE: Stress on the bones can be a good thing. Walking, jogging, and light aerobic exercise helps the bones get stronger by working against gravity, putting stress on the skeleton and rebuilding bone. While not necessarily bone building, swimming can be an excellent exercise for joints and muscles, and great for arthritis.

CUCUMBER GAZPACHO

No chopping necessary! Toss the ingredients into the food processor for a refreshing and marvelous mellow flavored twist to gazpacho.

Makes 6 (2/3-cup) servings

4 cucumbers, peeled, seeded and cut into chunks

1/2 cup coarsely chopped parsley

1/4 cup fresh mint leaves

1 bunch green onion, cut into pieces

1/2 small red onion, cut into chunks

3 tablespoons olive oil

2 tablespoons white wine vinegar

6 ounces Greek nonfat plain yogurt

1/2 cup walnuts, toasted

1 cup small ice cubes

Salt and pepper to taste

NUTRIENTS

Calories 175

Calories from Fat 68%

Fat 13g

Saturated Fat 2g

Cholesterol 0mg

Sodium 25mg

Carbohydrates 9g

Dietary Fiber 3g

Total Sugars 5g

Protein 5g

Dietary Exchanges: 2 vegetable, 2 1/2 fat

1. Combine all ingredients in blender; blend until smooth.

To seed cucumber, cut in half and run spoon down center of cucumber to easily remove seeds.

GOOD MORNING SMOOTHIE

Toss everyday ingredients into a blender for a morning pick-me-up.

Makes 4 (1-cup) servings

1 medium banana

1 cup orange juice

6 ounces low-fat vanilla yogurt

1 cup frozen strawberries

1. Combine all ingredients in food processor or blender until smooth. Pour into glasses.

NUTRIENTS

Calories 110

Calories from Fat 7%

Total Fat 1g

Saturated Fat 0g

Cholesterol 2mg

Sodium 29mg

Total Carbohydrate 24g

Dietary Fiber 2g

Sugars 17g

Protein 3g

Diabetic Exchanges: 1 Fruit, 1/2 Fat-Free Milk

STRAWBERRY FRUIT DIP

This luscious berry dip also makes a sensational soup or smoothie.

Makes 40 (1-tablespoon) servings

1 quart strawberries, stemmed and finely chopped

1/4 cup light brown sugar

1/4 cup orange juice

1 cup nonfat vanilla yogurt

1/2 teaspoon grated orange rind, optional

1. In bowl, mix all ingredients. Cover and refrigerate.

See page 84 for photo

NUTRIENTS

Calories 16

Calories from Fat 0%

Fat 0g

Saturated Fat 0g

Cholesterol 0mg

Sodium 5mg

Carbohydrate 4g

Dietary Fiber 0g

Sugar 3g

Protein 0g

Diabetic Exchanges: Free

SPINACH ARTICHOKE DIP

Quick and popular, here's one of my favorite spinach dip recipes that explodes with flavors of creamy Brie and Parmesan.

Makes 20 (1/4-cup) servings

1 onion, chopped

1/3 cup all-purpose flour

2 cups skim milk

1 teaspoon minced garlic

2 (10-ounce) boxes frozen chopped spinach, thawed and drained

4 ounces Brie cheese, rind removed and cubed

1/3 cup grated Parmesan cheese

1 (14-ounce) can artichoke hearts, drained and quartered

Salt and pepper to taste

1. In nonstick pot coated with nonstick cooking spray, sauté onion until tender. Stir in flour. Gradually add milk, stirring constantly, heating until bubbly and thickened.

2. Add garlic, spinach, Brie, and Parmesan cheese, stirring until cheese is melted. Stir in artichokes, and season to taste.

   D

NUTRIENTS

Calories 54

Calories from fat 34%

Fat 2g

Saturated Fat 1g

Cholesterol 7mg

Sodium 125mg

Carbohydrate 5g

Dietary Fiber 1g

Sugar 2g

Protein 4g

Dietary Exchanges: 1 vegetable, 1/2 fat

Try serving with assorted vegetables such as red pepper squares, cucumber, squash, and zucchini rounds.

Boost vitamin D intake by drinking low-fat milk, and spend 10-15 minutes a day in the sun — sunlight triggers vitamin D production in your body.

BOK CHOY SALAD

Introduce yourself to this versatile Chinese white cabbage, a leafy green vegetable, for this innovative salad that you will surprisingly adore.

Makes 6 servings

2 bunches baby bok choy, cleaned and chopped or sliced (about 6 cups)

1 bunch green onions, chopped

1/4 cup sliced almonds, toasted

1 (8-ounce) can mandarin oranges, drained

2 tablespoons olive oil

3 tablespoons seasoned rice or apple vinegar

1 tablespoon plus 1 teaspoon sugar

2 tablespoons low-sodium soy sauce

1. In large bowl, combine bok choy, green onion, almonds and mandarin oranges.
2. In small bowl, whisk together oil, vinegar, sugar and soy sauce. Toss salad with dressing.

NUTRIENTS

Calories 125

Calories from fat 46%

Fat 7g

Saturated Fat 1g

Cholesterol 0mg

Sodium 336mg

Carbohydrate 15g

Dietary Fiber 3g

Sugars 12g

Protein 2g

Dietary Exchanges: 1/2 fruit, 1 vegetable, 1 1/2 fat

TERRIFIC TIP

A fall/winter member of the cabbage family, the flavor of Bok Choy is mild and slightly sweet with a gentle hint of cabbage. 1 cup= only 30 calories and good source of vitamins C, A and calcium.

BROCCOLI SALAD WITH SESAME VINAIGRETTE

Sweet dried fruit, crunchy walnuts and toasty sesame seeds turn broccoli into a memorable salad.

Makes 6 (1-cup) servings

6 cups broccoli florets

1 tablespoon dried pomegranates or cranberries

1/4 cup coarsely chopped walnuts, toasted

1/4 cup chopped red onion

1 tablespoon sesame oil

3 tablespoons seasoned rice wine or apple vinegar

1/2 teaspoon minced garlic

Large pinch cayenne

2 teaspoons toasted sesame seeds

1. In microwave-safe dish, microwave broccoli in small amount of water 3-4 minutes or just until tender (bright green); drain.

2. In large bowl, combine cooked broccoli, dried pomegranates, walnuts and red onion.

3. In small bowl, whisk sesame oil, vinegar, garlic, and cayenne. Toss lightly with broccoli mixture. Sprinkle with toasted sesame seeds.

NUTRIENTS

Calories 104

Calories from Fat 50%

Fat 6g

Saturated Fat 1g

Cholesterol 0mg

Sodium 126mg

Carbohydrates 11g

Dietary Fiber 3g

Total Sugars 5g

Protein 4g

Dietary Exchanges: 2 vegetable, 1 fat

NUTRITIONAL
NUGGET

Did you know small little sesame seeds are full of bone-building calcium? Per tablespoon, whole sesame seeds contain about 88 mg of calcium.

ROASTED SALMON & BROCCOLI SALAD

Roasting, one-step cooking, enhances the flavor of salmon and broccoli.

Makes 5 (1-cup) servings

1 (16-ounce) salmon fillet

4 cups broccoli florets

2 teaspoons olive oil

Salt and pepper to taste

1 cup grape or cherry tomatoes, halved

1/3 cup chopped red onion

2 cups chopped cucumber

2 tablespoons chopped fresh basil or 2 teaspoons dried basil

Vinaigrette (recipe follows)

4 cups assorted mixed salad greens

1. Preheat oven 400°F. Cover baking pan with foil.
2. Place salmon on one side of pan and broccoli on other side. Toss broccoli with olive oil and season to taste. Roast 15-20 minutes, or until salmon is done. Cool salmon; flake with fork.
3. In large bowl, combine flaked salmon, roasted broccoli, tomatoes, onion, cucumber and basil. Toss with Vinaigrette (see recipe) and serve over mixed greens.

VINAIGRETTE

1 tablespoon olive oil

1/4 cup seasoned rice or white vinegar

1 tablespoon lemon juice

1 teaspoon Dijon mustard

1. In small bowl, whisk together all ingredients.

NUTRIENTS

Calories 224

Calories from Fat 36%

Fat 9g

Saturated Fat 1g

Cholesterol 42mg

Sodium 283mg

Carbohydrates 14g

Dietary Fiber 4g

Total Sugars 7g

Protein 23g

Dietary Exchanges: 2 vegetable, 3 lean meat

TERRIFIC TIP

Use leftover salmon to turn into this main dish salad.

Depending on salmon thickness roast about 10 minutes per inch.

NUTRITIONAL NUGGET

Broccoli contains a fair amount of calcium, but more importantly it is well absorbed by the body, and is an especially significant source for individuals that do not eat dairy.

SALMON WITH SPINACH FETA STUFFING

This simple and superb salmon is impressive to eat, and has become one of everyone's favorites.

Makes 4 servings

2 ounces reduced-fat cream cheese
1/2 cup crumbled reduced-fat feta cheese
1/3 cup chopped red onion
1/2 cup chopped baby spinach
4 (6-ounce) salmon fillets

1. Preheat oven 350°F. Coat baking dish with nonstick cooking spray.

2. In bowl, combine cream cheese and feta with fork, mixing until blended. Add onion and spinach, combining well.

3. Split each piece of salmon in half lengthwise without cutting all the way through (make pocket). Divide filling in each fillet spreading to cover. Place top salmon piece back over filling and on prepared baking dish.

4. Bake 20 minutes or until flaky and done.

NUTRIENTS

Calories 291
Calories from fat 37%
Fat 11g
Saturated Fat 4g
Cholesterol 114mg
Sodium 438mg
Carbohydrate 3g
Dietary Fiber 0g
Sugars 1g
Protein 42g
Dietary Exchanges: 5 lean meat

NUTRITIONAL NUGGET

Salmon is rich in omega-3 fatty acids, having a wide variety of benefits from reducing the risk of heart disease and stroke to reducing joint pain from inflammation – and is better absorbed through food than supplements.

Two cups of baby spinach pack over three times the daily recommended amount of bone-building vitamin k.

TEX-MEX TUNA TIDBITS WITH TROPICAL SALSA

D

NUTRIENTS

Calories 160
Calories from fat 4%
Fat 1g
Saturated Fat 0g
Cholesterol 37mg
Sodium 288mg
Carbohydrates 12g
Dietary Fiber 1g
Total Sugars 8g
Protein 25g
Dietary Exchanges: 1 fruit,
3 lean meat

Tuna is a good source of Vitamin D, which plays a major role in keeping strong bones by helping the body absorb calcium.

Southwestern seared tuna with cool yogurt sauce and Tropical Salsa.

Makes 6 servings

1 1/4 pounds fresh ahi tuna fillets, cut into 3/4-inch pieces
3 tablespoons taco seasoning
1/2 cup nonfat plain yogurt
1/2 teaspoon ground cumin
1/2 teaspoon chili powder
Tropical Salsa, (recipe follows)

1. In bowl, toss tuna with taco seasoning mix.
2. In nonstick skillet coated with nonstick cooking spray, add tuna and sear over medium-high heat and cook tuna 2-3 minutes or until desired doneness.
3. In bowl, mix yogurt, cumin and chili powder; set aside. Serve tuna with yogurt mixture, and Tropical Salsa (see recipe).

TROPICAL SALSA

Makes 6 (heaping 1/3-cup) servings

1 cup chopped mango
1 cup chopped pineapple
1/2 cup chopped cucumber
2 teaspoons chopped jalapeño peppers
1 tablespoon lime juice

1. In bowl, combine all ingredients. Refrigerate.

Lots of serving options: Serve in tacos, on mixed greens or with toothpicks as an appetizer or light meal.

CRABMEAT PASTA

Crabmeat and spinach pair up in this easy, exceptionally delicious dish.

Makes 8 (1-cup) servings

  D

8 ounces angel hair pasta (try whole grain)

1 tablespoon butter

1 tablespoon olive oil

1/2 pound sliced mushrooms

1/2 cup chopped green onion

1/3 cup chopped fresh parsley

1 teaspoon minced garlic

1 tablespoon cornstarch

1 (12-ounce) can fat-free evaporated skim milk, divided

1/3 cup white wine (or broth)

2 cups packed baby spinach leaves

1 pound back fin lump or white crabmeat, picked of shells

1//3 cup grated Parmesan cheese, optional

NUTRIENTS

Calories 248

Calories from Fat 17%

Fat 5g

Saturated Fat 1g

Cholesterol 49mg

Sodium 290mg

Carbohydrates 29g

Dietary Fiber 1g

Total Sugars 7g

Protein 21g

Dietary Exchanges: 1 1/2 starch, 1/2 fat-free skim milk, 2 lean meat

1. Cook pasta according to package directions. Drain; set aside.
2. In large nonstick skillet, heat butter and oil and sauté mushrooms, green onion, parsley, and garlic over medium heat about 5 minutes, or until tender.
3. In bowl, combine cornstarch with 1/2 cup evaporated milk, and mix until smooth. Add to pan and stir continuously.
4. Gradually add wine and remaining milk, stirring until mixture thickens. Reduce heat and add spinach and crabmeat, stirring until spinach wilted. Season to taste.
5. Toss with pasta and sprinkle with Parmesan cheese, if desired.

12 cups uncooked spinach equals 2 cups cooked — that's 12 cups of nutrients packed into 2!

Although not always budget-friendly, Shiitake mushrooms can be an excellent substitution for regular mushrooms as they have fiber and nutrients known to reduce cholesterol and inflammation.

CHICKEN, BROCCOLI, & RICE CASSEROLE

Chicken, broccoli and rice in a creamy cheese sauce is a basic real people pleaser recipe.

Makes 8 (1-cup) servings

1/4 cup all-purpose flour

2 1/2 cups skim milk

1 teaspoon minced garlic

1 teaspoon Dijon mustard

2 cups reduced-fat shredded sharp Cheddar cheese

3 cups cooked rice (brown preferred)

3 cups cooked broccoli florets

2 cups chopped or shredded cooked chicken breast

Salt and pepper to taste

1. Preheat oven 400°F. Coat 2-quart baking dish with nonstick cooking spray.
2. In nonstick pot, whisk together flour and milk. Cook on low heat, stirring constantly until thickened and bubbly. Whisk in garlic and Dijon; add cheese, stirring until melted.
3. Transfer rice, broccoli and chicken into baking dish; stir in cheese sauce, gently mix. Season to taste. Bake 20-30 minutes until bubbly and lightly golden on top.

NUTRIENTS

Calories 275

Calories from Fat 25%

Fat 8g

Saturated Fat 4g

Cholesterol 47mg

Sodium 292mg

Carbohydrates 27g

Dietary Fiber 2g

Total Sugars 5g

Protein 24g

Dietary Exchanges: 1 1/2 starch, 1/2 fat-free milk, 3 lean meat

Great for leftover chicken or can use rotisserie chicken. Use frozen or fresh broccoli florets and cook in microwave.

Try using brown rice to easily boost fiber: 1 cup rice equals less than 1g fiber while 1 cup brown rice equals 3g fiber.

SPINACH & CHEESE TORTILLA PIZZA

Easily turn tortillas into individual pizzas with these simple ingredients for a light lunch or snack.

Makes 12 (1-slice) servings

2 (10-inch) flour tortillas (corn tortillas for Gluten-free option)

Salt and pepper to taste

2 tablespoons Greek nonfat plain yogurt

1 (10-ounce) package frozen chopped spinach, thawed and squeezed dry

2 Roma tomatoes, chopped or 1 (14-ounce) can chopped fire-roasted tomatoes, drained

2/3 cup shredded reduced-fat Mexican blend cheese

1/4 cup chopped green onion

1. Preheat oven 450°F. Coat baking pan with nonstick cooking spray.
2. Place tortillas on prepared pan. Bake 3 minutes, or until golden brown. Remove from oven and reduce temperature 350°F.
3. Season yogurt and spread evenly over tortillas. Top with spinach and tomato. Sprinkle evenly with cheese.
4. Bake 5 minutes more, or until cheese is melted. Sprinkle with green onion. Cut each tortilla into 6 slices and serve.

NUTRIENTS

Calories 63

Calories from Fat 30%

Fat 2g

Saturated Fat 1g

Cholesterol 4mg

Sodium 173mg

Carbohydrates 8g

Dietary Fiber 1g

Total Sugars 1g

Protein 4g

Dietary Exchanges: 1/2 starch, 1/2 lean meat

NUTRITIONAL NUGGET

The rich green color in spinach is chocked full of nutrition — concentrated in phytonutrients and flavonoids, offering healthy antioxidant protection.

SPINACH & MUSHROOM PASTA

 D

Spinach and mushrooms join together in this fantastic light pasta.

Makes 4 servings

NUTRIENTS

Calories 280

Calories from Fat 25%

Fat 8g

Saturated Fat 1g

Cholesterol 0mg

Sodium 15mg

Carbohydrates 44g

Dietary Fiber 2g

Total Sugars 3g

Protein 9g

Dietary Exchanges: 3 starch, 1 fat

8 ounces thin spaghetti

2 tablespoons olive oil

1/4 pound sliced mushrooms

1 teaspoon minced garlic

1 1/2 cups baby spinach, packed

Dash red pepper flakes

2 tablespoons grated Parmesan cheese, optional

1. Cook pasta according to package directions. Drain; set aside.
2. Meanwhile, in large nonstick skillet, heat oil and sauté mushrooms and garlic until tender. Add spinach and red pepper, cooking just until spinach is wilted.
3. Add pasta and toss until heated. Sprinkle with cheese, if desired.

Use for vegetarian entrée or as a side to any meal.

Although calorie dense, a little olive oil goes a long way, working to block enzymes involved in inflammation — acting like ibuprofen.

MAC & CHEESE

One pot quick and creamy mac and cheese.

Makes 6 (3/4-cup) servings

2 cups dried small pasta (shells or elbow macaroni)
2 1/2 cups skim milk
6 slices reduced-fat American cheese
Salt to taste

1. In medium pot, combine pasta and milk. Bring to simmer, reduce heat to low and cook 20-25 minutes, until pasta is cooked, stirring frequently and don't let milk boil.
2. Turn off heat; add cheese and salt, stirring to combine.

See page 8 for photo

NUTRIENTS
Calories 235
Calories from Fat 22%
Fat 6g
Saturated Fat 3g
Cholesterol 17mg
Sodium 355mg
Carbohydrates 32g
Dietary Fiber 1g
Total Sugars 7g
Protein 13g
Dietary Exchanges: 2 starch, 1 1/2 lean meat

KALE CHIPS

Crisp and crunchy; melts in your mouth. No-fuss, simple, fun recipe.

Makes 8 servings

1 bunch of curly kale, washed, dried, torn into 2-inch pieces
Salt to taste

1. Preheat oven 400°F. Line baking pan with foil and coat with nonstick cooking spray.
2. Spread kale on prepared pan in single layer. Coat kale lightly with nonstick cooking spray. Season to taste.
3. Bake 8-10 minutes or until kale is crispy and edges brown.

NUTRIENTS
Calories 19
Calories from Fat 0
Fat 0g
Saturated Fat 0g
Cholesterol 0mg
Sodium 17mg
Carbohydrates 4g
Dietary Fiber 1g
Total Sugars 0g
Protein 1g
Dietary Exchanges: Free

BROCCOLI WITH WALNUTS

 **G D**

NUTRIENTS

Calories 111

Calories from Fat 56%

Fat 8g

Saturated Fat 1g

Cholesterol 2mg

Sodium 67mg

Carbohydrates 9g

Dietary Fiber 3g

Total Sugars 2g

Protein 5g

Dietary Exchanges: 2 vegetable, 1 1/2 fat

Broccoli and cauliflower have nutrients that may add protection from certain cancers, including breast cancer.

Simple ingredients transform broccoli into something spectacular.

Makes 8 (1-cup) servings

2 tablespoons olive oil

10 cups broccoli florets

Salt and pepper to taste

1 teaspoon minced garlic

1/3 cup coarsely chopped walnuts

2 tablespoons lemon juice

1/4 teaspoon red pepper flakes

3 tablespoons grated Parmesan cheese

1. In large nonstick skillet, heat oil and cook broccoli over medium-high heat until begins to get tender. Season to taste.

2. Add garlic and walnuts; cook until broccoli is crisp tender and walnuts are toasted. Toss with lemon juice, red pepper flakes and Parmesan.

CORNBREAD

Cornbread fans will relish this loaded moist cornbread packed with wonderful savory extras.

Makes 28 servings

1 1/2 cups yellow cornmeal

1/2 cup all-purpose flour

1/2 teaspoon baking soda

2 tablespoons sugar

1 cup skim milk

1 egg

1/4 cup canola oil

1 onion, chopped

1 green bell pepper, cored and chopped

1 (15-ounce) can cream-style corn

1 cup shredded reduced-fat sharp Cheddar cheese

1 bunch green onions, chopped

1. Preheat oven 350°F. Coat 13x9x2-inch pan with nonstick cooking spray.
2. In large bowl, combine cornmeal, flour, baking soda, and sugar.
3. In another bowl, combine milk, egg, and oil. Add remaining ingredients; mix well. Stir into flour mixture. Transfer to prepared pan. Bake 40-45 minutes or until golden brown.

NUTRIENTS

Calories 86

Calories from Fat 32%

Total Fat 3g

Saturated Fat 1g

Cholesterol 9mg

Sodium 99mg

Carbohydrate 12g

Fiber 1g

Sugar 2g

Protein 3g

Dietary Exchanges: 1 Starch, 1/2 Fat

Make in cupcake holders for individual servings.

Calcium and vitamin D are its most praised nutrients but skim milk is rich in potassium, protein and other nutrients needed to build our bones, as well.

Simple Sausage Ratatouille (pg 118)

5

FILL UP *with* FIBER

Dietary fiber is a form of complex carbohydrate that our gastrointestinal system does not digest or break down, therefore it helps food move through the body efficiently, aiding in healthy bowel function. Foods that are high in fiber get absorbed slowly into our system, therefore reducing spikes in blood sugar. Found naturally in plants, often the foods we know to be healthy are high in fiber, such as vegetables, fruits, and whole grains.

WHAT ARE THE TYPES OF FIBER?

There are two types of dietary fiber, soluble and insoluble – each with their own health benefits. Soluble fiber is named so because it dissolves in water, forming a gel-like consistency, keeping stool soft. For the most part, insoluble fiber stays in tact and passes through the digestive system absorbing water. Like a laxative, insoluble fiber helps prevent constipation and speed up food movement through the digestive system.

FOODS HIGH IN SOLUBLE FIBER:

- Barley
- Beans and Lentils
- Flax
- Nuts and Seeds
- Oatmeal
- Oat bran
- Fruits: apples, bananas, berries, pears, plums
- Vegetables: broccoli, carrots, potatoes, sweet potatoes, onions, dried peas

FOODS HIGH IN INSOLUBLE FIBER:

- Brown rice*
- Couscous
- Fruit: raisins, grapes
- Wheat bran and whole wheat
- Whole grains
- Vegetables: celery, broccoli, cabbage, onions, tomatoes, carrots, cucumbers, green beans, dark leafy vegetables, zucchini

*Substitute brown rice for white rice:
1 cup white rice = 1g fiber, 1 cup brown rice = 3g fiber

HOW MUCH FIBER IS RECOMMENDED TO EAT?

According to the Dietary Guidelines for Americans, 25 grams of fiber is the recommended daily amount for women and 38 grams for men. After age 50, the need drops to 21 grams daily for women and 30 grams for men. The health benefits of consuming the recommended amount of fiber are numerous, including heart health, reducing cholesterol, and even decreasing the risk of some cancers. Because of the laxative effect, fiber helps reduce digestive problems such as constipation, as well as helping to keep a healthy weight. Weight maintenance is important for those suffering with arthritis as extra body weight bears extra pressure on the joints. Losing unneeded weight will help alleviate pain from this extra pressure, especially in hip and knee joints. Because high fiber foods are often low fat, low calorie foods they provide bulk in the diet, helping one feel full without extra calories.

WHY EAT FIBER?

Fiber may be helpful for those with arthritis for more than just weight maintenance. CRP or C-reactive protein is found in the blood as an indicator of inflammation, with higher levels of CRP indicating inflammation in the body. Research has found that diets high in fiber (the recommended daily amount) reduced CRP levels, therefore reducing inflammation.

Found naturally in plants, often the foods we know to be healthy are high in fiber, such as vegetables, fruits, and whole grains.

BEST BARLEY SOUP

Barley soup at its best with salty bacon, naturally sweet yams, earthy mushrooms and carrots. In the mood for a heartier soup, just add meat.

Makes 11 (1-cup) servings

 D

5 slices turkey bacon

1/2 pound sliced mushrooms

1 teaspoon minced garlic

1 red onion, chopped

1/2 teaspoon dried thyme leaves

8 cups low-sodium fat-free chicken broth

2 cups chopped carrots

2 cups chopped Louisiana yams (sweet potatoes), peeled and cut into small cubes

3/4 cup medium pearl barley

1. In large nonstick pot, cook bacon until crisp. Remove to paper towels, crumble, set aside.

2. In same pot coated with nonstick cooking spray, sauté mushrooms, garlic, and onion until tender about 7 minutes.

3. Add thyme, broth, carrots, sweet potatoes and barley. Bring to boil, reduce heat, cover, and cook 25 minutes or until barley and vegetables are tender. Season to taste. To serve, sprinkle with crumbled bacon.

NUTRIENTS

Calories 108

Calories from Fat 8%

Fat 1g

Saturated Fat 0g

Cholesterol 5mg

Sodium 137mg

Carbohydrates 20g

Dietary Fiber 4g

Total Sugars 3g

Protein 5g

Dietary Exchanges: 1 starch, 1 vegetable

For vegetarian option, omit bacon and use vegetable broth.

If soup gets too thick, add more broth.

With a nut-like flavor and pasta-like consistency, barley is an excellent fiber-rich grain, also high in selenium which helps play a role in protecting inflammation.

QUICK VEGGIE SOUP

Keep it convenient with frozen and canned ingredients for a classic and colorful mild tomato tasting vegetable soup.

Makes 8 (1-cup) servings

NUTRIENTS

Calories 119

Calories from Fat 8%

Fat 1g

Saturated Fat 0g

Cholesterol 0mg

Sodium 348mg

Carbohydrates 26g

Dietary Fiber 4g

Total Sugars 8g

Protein 3g

Dietary Exchanges: 1 starch, 1 vegetable

1/2 cup chopped onion

1 teaspoon minced garlic

3 cups low-sodium fat-free vegetable or chicken broth

1 (16-ounce) bag frozen mixed vegetables

1 (14 3/4-ounce) can cream-style corn

1 (14-ounce) can chopped fire-roasted tomatoes

1 tablespoon Worcestershire sauce

1/4 cup rice

Salt and pepper to taste

1. In large nonstick pot coated with nonstick cooking spray, sauté onion and garlic until tender, about 5 minutes.

2. Add broth, frozen vegetables, cream style corn, tomatoes and Worcestershire sauce. Bring to boil, add rice and reduce heat; cook 15 minutes. Season to taste.

TERRIFIC TIP

Try adding chopped fresh Louisiana yams for a boost of natural sweetness and nutrition.

BLACK BEAN SOUP

Take a short-cut with canned beans and southwestern seasonings for an amazing soup. Go Cuban and serve with rice and chopped onion.

Makes 8 (1-cup) servings

1 onion, chopped

1 green bell pepper, cored and chopped

1 teaspoon minced garlic

1 (14 1/2-ounce) can chopped fire-roasted tomatoes with juice

1 (4-ounce) can chopped green chilies

1 teaspoon ground cumin

1 teaspoon chili powder

4 (15-ounce) cans black beans, rinsed and drained

4 cups low-sodium fat-free vegetable broth

Salt and pepper to taste

1. In large pot coated with nonstick cooking spray, sauté onion, green pepper, and garlic until tender, 7 minutes.
2. Add tomatoes with juice, green chilies, cumin, and chili powder. Gradually add black beans and broth.
3. Remove 2 cups of black bean mixture, puree in processor or blender until smooth.
4. Return pureed mixture to pot, bring to boil. Lower heat, simmer 10–15 minutes. Season to taste.

NUTRIENTS

Calories 212

Calories from fat 8%

Fat 2g

Saturated Fat 0g

Cholesterol 0mg

Sodium 576mg

Carbohydrate 34g

Dietary Fiber 14g

Sugars 3g

Protein 13g

Diabetic Exchanges: 2 starch, 1 vegetable, 1 very lean meat

Always rinse canned beans to lower sodium content.

A nutritional bargain, beans provide an excellent source of fiber and folate, helping with digestive health and weight maintenance.

SPINACH SALAD WITH PROSCIUTTO & MELON

Fresh and fabulous, prosciutto, melon, avocado and crunchy walnuts tossed with spinach and a Dijon vinaigrette will "wow" you!

Makes 6 servings

8 cups baby spinach

3 ounces prosciutto, chopped

2 cups cubed cantaloupe (1-inch pieces)

1/2 cup diced red onion

1 avocado, diced

1/3 cup coarsely chopped walnuts

Dijon Vinaigrette, (recipe follows)

1. In large bowl combine all ingredients and toss with Dijon Vinaigrette (see recipe).

DIJON VINAIGRETTE

1 tablespoon Dijon mustard

3 tablespoons lemon juice

3 tablespoons olive oil

2 tablespoons balsamic vinegar

Salt and pepper to taste

1. In small bowl, whisk together all ingredients.

NUTRIENTS

Calories 234

Calories from Fat 67%

Fat 18g

Saturated Fat 3g

Cholesterol 12mg

Sodium 349mg

Carbohydrates 13g

Dietary Fiber 4g

Total Sugars 7g

Protein 7g

Dietary Exchanges: 1/2 fruit, 1 vegetable, 1/2 lean meat, 3 fat

Along with fiber, spinach is rich in antioxidants providing excellent anti-inflammatory benefits.

HUMMUS & TABBOULEH SALAD

A layered mound of fantastic flavors makes a splendid Mediterranean salad. Serve with toasted pita bread. Also, makes a great dip.

Makes 4 (1-cup) servings

1 (5.25-ounce) box Tabbouleh mix wheat salad (makes 2 1/2 cups)

1 tablespoon olive oil

1/2 cup chopped red onion

1 cup chopped tomatoes

1 cup finely chopped cucumber

1/3 cup chopped fresh parsley (flat leaf preferred)

2 tablespoons lemon juice

Salt and pepper to taste

1 (10-ounce) container roasted red pepper hummus

1/4 cup crumbled reduced-fat feta cheese

1. In bowl, prepare Tabbouleh mix according to package instructions. Refrigerate covered with plastic wrap. After water absorbed, fluff with fork and add olive oil, mixing well.

2. To Tabbouleh, add red onion, tomatoes, cucumber, parsley, lemon juice and season to taste.

3. On large serving plate, spread hummus, top with Tabbouleh salad and sprinkle with feta. Refrigerate until serving.

NUTRIENTS

Calories 308

Calories from Fat 34%

Fat 12g

Saturated Fat 1g

Cholesterol 3mg

Sodium 909mg

Carbohydrates 47g

Dietary Fiber 11g

Total Sugars 7g

Protein 9g

Dietary Exchanges: 3 starch, 2 fat

TERRIFIC TIP

Tabbouleh is a salad made with bulgur, a nutty tasty cracked wheat high in fiber, easily prepared by pouring hot water over the bulgur in a bowl.

NUTRITIONAL NUGGET

Parsley is a good source of plant iron. One cup contains about 20% of your RDA.

BRUSSELS SPROUTS, TOMATO & FETA SALAD

 **G D**

A remarkable combination with just a few ingredients. If you've never had fresh Brussels sprouts, I promise this recipe will win you over.

Make 8 (2/3-cup) servings

1 1/4 pounds fresh Brussels sprouts

2 teaspoons plus 3 tablespoons olive oil

1/4 cup white balsamic vinegar

1 tablespoon Dijon mustard

Salt and pepper to taste

1 cup grape or cherry tomatoes, halved

1/3 cup crumbled reduced-fat feta cheese

3 tablespoons chopped green onions

1. Preheat oven 450°F. Line baking pan with foil and coat with nonstick cooking spray.

2. Remove outer discolored leaves from Brussels sprouts and cut in half. Place on prepared pan and drizzle with 2 teaspoons oil, tossing. Bake 20- 25 minutes or until tender. Cool.

3. In small bowl, whisk together vinegar, Dijon, remaining 3 tablespoons oil, and season to taste.

4. In bowl, combine Brussels sprouts, tomatoes and feta; toss with vinaigrette and green onion.

NUTRIENTS

Calories 113

Calories from Fat 55%

Fat 7g

Saturated Fat 1g

Cholesterol 2mg

Sodium 141mg

Carbohydrates 10g

Dietary Fiber 3g

Total Sugars 4g

Protein 4g

Dietary Exchanges: 2 vegetable, 1 1/2 fat

TERRIFIC TIP

If you do not have or cannot find white balsamic vinegar, any vinegar may be used.

NUTRITIONAL NUGGET

Brussels sprouts provide awesome DNA protective and cancer preventative benefits so keep them on your weekly menu.

BRUSCHETTA COUSCOUS SALAD

All the components of bruschetta tossed with couscous is about as good as it gets! I recommend using fresh mozzarella and basil in this salad.

Makes 7 (1-cup) servings

1 1/2 cups Israeli couscous

1/2 cup chopped red onion

2 cups cherry or grape tomato halves

1 cup chopped cucumber

1 cup small fresh mozzarella balls or pieces (fresh mozzarella is best)

1/3 cup fresh basil leaves, torn into pieces or 2 tablespoons dried basil leaves

3 tablespoons olive oil

2 tablespoons grated Parmesan cheese, optional

2 tablespoons balsamic vinegar

1 teaspoon minced garlic

Salt and pepper to taste

1. Cook couscous according to package directions. Fluff with fork and cool.
2. In large bowl, combine couscous, red onion, tomatoes, cucumber, mozzarella and basil. In small bowl, whisk together remaining ingredients and toss with couscous mixture.

NUTRIENTS

Calories 267

Calories from Fat 35%

Fat 10g

Saturated Fat 3g

Cholesterol 14mg

Sodium 43mg

Carbohydrates 34g

Dietary Fiber 3g

Total Sugars 4g

Protein 9g

Dietary Exchanges: 2 starch, 1 vegetable, 1/2 lean meat, 1 fat

You know you are eating with nutrition when you have this colorful of a plate — each color providing important protective vitamins and nutrients.

Instead of couscous, wild rice may be used for Gluten-free version.

Don't have Israeli couscous, just use what you have.

FESTIVE QUINOA SALAD

 **D**

Fresh ingredients like cucumber and mint join hearty quinoa, tart cranberries and crunchy almonds for an energizing colorful combination.

NUTRIENTS

Calories 225

Calories from Fat 29%

Fat 7g

Saturated Fat 1g

Cholesterol 0mg

Sodium 72mg

Carbohydrates 34g

Dietary Fiber 4g

Total Sugars 10g

Protein 7g

Dietary Exchanges: 2 starch, 1/2 fruit, 1 fat

If you have never tried quinoa, make sure you do, as this grain-like seed is a special source high in protein, low in fat and also contains iron and fiber – especially important for vegetarians.

Makes 5 (1-cup) servings

1 cup quinoa, rinsed and drained well

2 cups water

1/4 cup white balsamic vinegar

3 tablespoons lime juice

1 tablespoon olive oil

1 tablespoon Dijon mustard

1/4 teaspoon dried Italian seasoning

1 1/2 cups diced peeled cucumber

1/2 cup chopped red onion

1/4 cup coarsely chopped almonds, toasted

1/4 cup dried cranberries

2 tablespoons chopped fresh mint

Salt and pepper to taste

1. In medium pot, combine quinoa and water. Bring to boil, cover, and reduce heat. Simmer 10-15 minutes. Cool.

2. In small bowl, whisk together white balsamic vinegar, lime juice, olive oil, mustard, and Italian seasoning; set aside.

3. In large bowl, combine quinoa, cucumber, onion, almonds, cranberries and mint. Pour dressing over quinoa mixture, tossing gently. Season to taste.

BLACK BEAN & MANGO SALAD

A colorful concoction bursting with fresh flavors tossed in a zingy vinaigrette. Add 1/2 teaspoon ginger to spice it up.

Makes about 6 (1/2-cup) servings

1 (15-ounce) can black beans, rinsed and drained

1 cup chopped mango

1/2 cup chopped red onion

1 avocado, chopped

2 tablespoons lime juice

1 teaspoon light brown sugar

Dash red pepper flakes

1. In medium bowl, combine all ingredients. Refrigerate until serving.

NUTRIENTS

Calories 141

Calories from fat 35%

Fat 6g

Saturated Fat 1g

Cholesterol 0mg

Sodium 222mg

Carbohydrate 19g

Dietary Fiber 7g

Sugars 6g

Protein 5g

Diabetic Exchanges: 1 starch, 1/2 fruit, 1 fat

TERRIFIC TIP

If mangos aren't in season, they may be found in jars, cans or frozen in the grocery.

NUTRITIONAL NUGGET

Beans are a nutritional high fiber bargain, aiding in weight maintenance — and by rinsing and draining the canned variety you will reduce the sodium by 40%!

CHICKEN TACO RICE SALAD

A favorite toss-together southwestern style chef salad with simple ingredients and big flavor.

Makes 6 (2-cup) servings

1 (5-ounce) package yellow rice

6 cups mixed salad greens

2 cups skinless rotisserie chicken, shredded

1 (15-ounce) can black beans, rinsed and drained

1 cup grape or cherry tomato halves

1/2 cup chopped red onion

1/2 cup shredded, reduced-fat, sharp Cheddar cheese

Salsa Vinaigrette, (recipe follows)

1. Prepare rice according to package directions. Cool; set aside.
2. In large bowl, combine cooled rice and all ingredients. Serve with Salsa Vinaigrette (see recipe).

SALSA VINAIGRETTE

Makes 1 1/2 cups

1 cup salsa

2 teaspoons chili powder

1/2 teaspoon ground cumin

1 tablespoon lime juice

2 tablespoons olive oil

1. In small bowl, whisk together all ingredients.

NUTRIENTS

Calories 327

Calories from Fat 29%

Fat 11g

Saturated Fat 3g

Cholesterol 57mg

Sodium 923mg

Carbohydrates 36g

Dietary Fiber 6g

Total Sugars 4g

Protein 23g

Dietary Exchanges: 2 starch, 1 vegetable, 2 1/2 lean meat

Think of beans as the nutritional crouton, sprinkle on salads or in casseroles and soups to boost your fiber intake.

Only use the amount of vinaigrette you desire; save remainder for another time.

SMOKED SALMON QUINOA SALAD

Sweet, savory, and salty in one marvelous bite. Turn this salad into your own creation or go vegetarian by omitting the salmon or adding your favorite fresh vegetables.

Makes 5 (1-cup) servings

3 cups cooked quinoa (or can use couscous)

2 ounces smoked salmon, cut into small pieces

1/2 cup frozen corn, thawed

1/2 cup chopped red onion

1/3 cup dried cranberries

1/4 cup pumpkin seeds

1 tablespoon plus 1 teaspoon olive oil

2 tablespoons lemon juice

Salt and pepper to taste

1. In large bowl, combine quinoa, smoked salmon, corn, onion, cranberries, pumpkin seeds and 1 tablespoon olive oil.

2. In small bowl, whisk together remaining 1 teaspoon olive oil and lemon juice. Toss with quinoa mixture and season to taste.

NUTRIENTS

Calories 275

Calories from Fat 31%

Fat 10g

Saturated Fat 1g

Cholesterol 11mg

Sodium 78mg

Carbohydrates 37g

Dietary Fiber 4g

Total Sugars 8g

Protein 12g

Dietary Exchanges: 2 starch, 1/2 fruit, 1 lean meat, 1 fat

TERRIFIC TIP

If you haven't tried quinoa, you will enjoy the easy preparation and terrific taste of this nutty grain.

SHRIMP TOSS WITH ASPARAGUS & WHITE BEANS

A trouble-free toss together dish with shrimp, asparagus and white beans in a light sauce. Serve over pasta, rice or couscous.

Makes 4 (1 1/4-cup) servings

1 tablespoon olive oil

1 pound asparagus, trimmed and cut into 1-inch pieces

1 tablespoon minced garlic

1 pound medium shrimp, peeled

1 (14-ounce) can chopped fire-roasted tomatoes, drained

1 (15-ounce) can navy beans, rinsed and drained

1 cup low-sodium fat-free chicken broth

2 teaspoons cornstarch

1/2 teaspoon dried basil leaves

Salt and pepper to taste

Grated Parmesan cheese, optional

1. In large nonstick skillet, heat oil over medium-high heat; cook asparagus and garlic 1 - 2 minutes, stirring.

2. Add shrimp and cook until almost done, 3-5 minutes. Add tomatoes and beans, stirring.

3. In small bowl, mix together broth and cornstarch, stir into skillet. Cook over medium heat until thickened, stirring frequently. Add basil, season to taste, and sprinkle with cheese, if desired.

NUTRIENTS

Calories 287

Calories from Fat 16%

Fat 5g

Saturated Fat 1g

Cholesterol 143mg

Sodium 931mg

Carbohydrates 34g

Dietary Fiber 9g

Total Sugars 7g

Protein 27g

Dietary Exchanges: 1 1/2 starch, 2 vegetable, 3 lean meat

TERRIFIC TIP

You can substitute chicken but cook chicken first in skillet in oil and proceed with recipe adding asparagus.

NUTRITIONAL NUGGET

Asparagus provides a great source of vitamins A, B6, C, E. High sodium in this recipe keeps it from being diabetic-friendly. Use no-salt tomatoes and look for low-sodium beans.

SOUTHWESTERN BEEF CASSEROLE WITH SWEET POTATO TOPPING

A fast-fix meaty one-dish delicious dinner made with pantry friendly ingredients.

Makes 6 servings

1 pound ground sirloin

1 (15-ounce) can black beans, drained and rinsed

1 (14 1/2-ounce) can chopped fire-roasted tomatoes

1 cup frozen corn, thawed

1 (10-ounce) can 98% fat-free cream of chicken soup

2 cups frozen sweet potato tater tots or waffle cut

1. Preheat oven 375°F. Coat 9x9x2-inch square baking dish with nonstick cooking spray.

2. In large skillet, cook meat until done; drain any excess liquid.

3. Add black beans, tomatoes, and corn to pan, mixing well. Transfer to prepared pan.

4. Cover meat mixture evenly with cream of chicken soup and top with sweet potato waffles or tater tots. Bake 30-35 minutes or until tater tots are done and casserole is bubbly.

NUTRIENTS

Calories 326

Calories from fat 25%

Fat 9g

Saturated Fat 3g

Cholesterol 48mg

Sodium 611mg

Carbohydrate 37g

Dietary Fiber 6g

Sugars 10g

Protein 23g

Dietary Exchanges: 2 1/2 starch, 2 lean meat, 1 fat

Use electronic appliances such as a can opener when possible for ease on joints.

SIMPLE SAUSAGE RATATOUILLE

Presto! Toss together sausage, squash, tomatoes, Italian seasonings and pasta for an outstanding dinner.

Makes 4 (1 1/4-cup) servings

8 ounces penne pasta

16 ounces chicken sausage, diced

2 cups coarsely chopped zucchini

2 cups coarsely chopped yellow squash

2 cups chopped onion

1 tablespoon minced garlic

1/2 cup low-sodium fat-free chicken broth

2 cups chopped tomatoes

1 teaspoon dried oregano leaves

1 teaspoon dried basil leaves

1. Cook pasta according to package directions. Drain and set aside.

2. In nonstick skillet, cook sausage over medium heat until browned, stirring. Add zucchini, squash, onion and garlic; sauté 5 minutes. Add broth, cooking until liquid is almost reduced.

3. Add tomatoes, oregano and basil, and cook until tomatoes tender. Serve over pasta.

NUTRIENTS

Calories 449

Calories from Fat 21%

Fat 10g

Saturated Fat 3g

Cholesterol 88mg

Sodium 631mg

Carbohydrates 60g

Dietary Fiber 5g

Total Sugars 10g

Protein 30g

Dietary Exchanges: 3 starch, 3 vegetable, 3 lean meat

Canned tomatoes, drained, may be substituted for fresh tomatoes.

SWEET POTATO & BLACK BEAN ENCHILADAS

Naturally "sweet" sweet potatoes and southwestern seasonings in a mild green enchilada sauce make an outrageously delicious enchilada.

Makes 12 enchiladas

2 large Louisiana yams, (sweet potatoes), peeled and cut into small cubes (4 cups)

1 green bell pepper, cored and chopped

1 red onion, chopped

1 teaspoon ground cumin

1 teaspoon chili powder

Salt and pepper to taste

1 (15-ounce) can black beans, rinsed and drained

2 teaspoons lime juice

1 1/2 cups green enchilada sauce, divided

12 flour tortillas (use corn tortillas for Gluten-free option)

1 1/2 cups reduced-fat shredded sharp Cheddar cheese

1. Preheat oven 425°F. Line baking pan with foil and coat with nonstick cooking spray.

2. Combine sweet potatoes, green pepper, onion, cumin, chili powder and season to taste on prepared pan. Roast 20-25 minutes or until fork tender. Add black beans and lime juice.

3. Reduce oven 350°F. Coat 2-quart baking dish with nonstick cooking spray. Spread 1/2 cup enchilada sauce on bottom of dish. In each tortilla, place heaping 1/3 cup sweet potato filling, and 1 tablespoon cheese. Roll up and place in baking dish, seam side down. Repeat with remaining tortillas.

4. Cover with remaining green enchilada sauce and sprinkle with remaining cheese. Bake 15 minutes or until heated and cheese melted.

NUTRIENTS

Calories 255

Calories from Fat 19%

Fat 5g

Saturated Fat 2g

Cholesterol 8mg

Sodium 742mg

Carbohydrates 42g

Dietary Fiber 7g

Total Sugars 6g

Protein 11g

Dietary Exchanges: 3 starch, 1/2 lean meat

NUTRITIONAL NUGGET

With little fat and low in sodium, sweet potatoes provide a delicious dose of fiber and vitamins A, C and E.

SOUTHWESTERN BAKED SWEET POTATOES

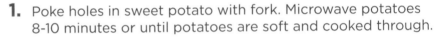

Layers of flavors explode into an exceptionally delicious sweet potato.

Makes 4 potatoes

NUTRIENTS

Calories 372

Calories from Fat 12%

Fat 5g

Saturated Fat 2g

Cholesterol 9mg

Sodium 567mg

Carbohydrates 66g

Dietary Fiber 14g

Total Sugars 13g

Protein 16g

Dietary Exchanges: 4 starch, 1 vegetable, 1 lean meat

4 medium sized Louisiana yams (sweet potatoes)

1/2 cup Greek nonfat plain yogurt

1 1/2 teaspoons chili powder, divided

1 teaspoon ground cumin, divided

Dash salt

1 teaspoon olive oil

1 red bell pepper, cored and chopped

1/2 red onion, diced

1/2 teaspoon paprika

1 (15-ounce) can black beans, rinsed and drained

1/2 cup reduced-fat shredded Mexican blend cheese

1/4 cup chopped green onion

1. Poke holes in sweet potato with fork. Microwave potatoes 8-10 minutes or until potatoes are soft and cooked through.
2. In small bowl, mix together yogurt, 1/2 teaspoon chili powder, 1/2 teaspoon cumin, and salt; set aside.
3. In small nonstick skillet, heat oil and sauté bell pepper, onion, remaining 1 teaspoon chili powder, remaining 1/2 teaspoon cumin and paprika until onion is slightly caramelized, about 5 minutes. Stir in black beans until heated.
4. Cut thin slice off top of potato and open wider by squeezing potato. Top each potato with cheese, black bean mixture, yogurt mixture and green onion.

TERRIFIC TIP

If you would rather, bake potatoes in oven at 400°F. about 1 hour.

NUTRITIONAL NUGGET

You know sweet potatoes are rich in vitamin A and carotenoids by their rich orange color – providing powerful anti-inflammatory antioxidants.

CHICKEN ENCHILADAS

An easy 'combine and stir' enchilada recipe with green enchilada sauce and a creamy chicken filling makes scrumptious, lighter style enchiladas.

12 enchiladas

6 ounces reduced-fat cream cheese

3 cups chopped, cooked chicken breasts

1 (4-ounce) can chopped green chilies

1 (28-ounce) can green enchilada sauce, divided

1 teaspoon chili powder

1 cup chopped green onion

12 (8-inch) flour tortillas (use corn tortillas for Gluten-free)

1 (15-ounce) can black beans, rinsed and drained

1 1/2 cups reduced-fat shredded Mexican blend cheese, divided

Chopped green onion, garnish

1. Preheat oven 350°F. Coat oblong 3-quart baking dish with nonstick cooking spray.

2. In microwave-safe dish, microwave cream cheese until melted (1 minute). In bowl, combine melted cream cheese, chicken, green chilies, 2 cups enchilada sauce, chili powder, and green onion.

3. Pour 1/2 cup remaining enchilada sauce in prepared baking dish. Spoon about 1/3 cup chicken mixture in each tortilla, some black beans and 1 tablespoon cheese. Roll up and place seam-side down in prepared baking dish. Repeat with remaining tortillas. Top with remaining enchilada sauce.

4. Cover with foil. Bake 25-30 minutes or until hot. Sprinkle with remaining cheese and return to oven until cheese melts, about 5 minutes. Sprinkle with green onion, if desired.

NUTRIENTS

Calories 323

Calories from Fat 30%

Fat 11g

Saturated Fat 4g

Cholesterol 49mg

Sodium 1047mg

Carbohydrates 35g

Dietary Fiber 5g

Total Sugars 5g

Protein 22g

Dietary Exchanges: 2 starch, 1 vegetable, 2 1/2 lean meat

TERRIFIC TIP

Look in the produce section of the grocery for containers of pre-chopped green onion.

Use corn tortillas for Gluten-free recipe.

Artichoke Squares (pg 126)

6

TOSS *the* FORK

It is natural for healthy people to eat and not think of every motion required. But for those suffering with arthritis, everyday ordinary tasks can be difficult. Some joints used more often tend to have a higher risk of developing arthritis especially in the hands. When it comes to fine motor skills involving food preparation, even holding utensils such as forks, knives and spoons this can be increasingly difficult to maneuver. This chapter is here to alleviate a bit of that difficulty in holding small objects and fine motor control of using utensils – tossing the fork! These meals are adapted to reduce joint stress and increase leverage when gripping foods, making meals easier to hold and grip, including delicious and nutritious sandwiches, wraps and pizza slices.

This chapter is here to alleviate a bit of that difficulty in holding small objects and fine motor control of using utensils – tossing the fork!

Spinach and Artichoke White Pizza (pg 129)

Beefy Crescents (pg 137)

OPEN FACE BREAKFAST ENGLISH MUFFINS

Western omelet ingredients piled on an English muffin make this an ideal grab and go satisfying breakfast. Egg beaters may be substituted for egg and egg white combination.

Makes 6 muffins

1/2 cup chopped Canadian bacon

1/4 cup chopped onion

1/4 cup chopped green bell pepper

1/3 cup chopped tomatoes

2 eggs

5 egg whites

Salt and pepper to taste

3 whole wheat English muffins, halved

1/4 cup reduced-fat shredded Cheddar cheese

1. In nonstick skillet coated with nonstick cooking spray, cook Canadian bacon 2 minutes or until begins to brown. Add onion and, green pepper sautéing until tender. Add tomatoes, cook 1 minute. Remove from pan, set aside.

2. In small bowl, whisk together eggs and egg whites. In same nonstick skillet coated with nonstick cooking spray, scramble eggs. Season to taste. When eggs are almost done, stir in Canadian bacon-onion mixture.

3. Meanwhile, toast muffin halves. Divide egg mixture to top muffin halves. Sprinkle with cheese.

 D

NUTRIENTS

Calories 143

Calories from Fat 25%

Fat 4g

Saturated Fat 1g

Cholesterol 71mg

Sodium 391mg

Carbohydrates 15g

Dietary Fiber 3g

Total Sugars 4g

Protein 12g

Dietary Exchanges:
1 starch, 1 1/2 lean meat

To make ahead, the prepared muffins may be refrigerated and reheated in the microwave or in oven preheated at 350°F. about 5 minutes or until well heated.

Be sure to look for omega-3 fortified eggs to cook and bake with for an extra dose of heart-healthy protection and reduction in inflammation.

ARTICHOKE SQUARES

  D

These tasty squares make a great snack or hors' dóeuvre.

Makes 30 squares

1 cup chopped onion

1 cup chopped red bell pepper

1 cup chopped green bell pepper

1 cup sliced mushrooms

1 teaspoon minced garlic

2 (14-ounce) cans artichokes drained and chopped

3 egg whites, slightly beaten

2 eggs, slightly beaten

1 teaspoon dried oregano leaves

1 teaspoon dried basil leaves

1/4 teaspoon cayenne pepper

1/2 cup Italian bread crumbs

3/4 cup shredded reduced-fat sharp Cheddar cheese

1/4 cup grated Parmesan cheese

1. Preheat oven 350°F. Coat 2-quart oblong baking dish with nonstick cooking spray.

2. In medium pan coated with nonstick cooking spray, sauté onion, red and green pepper, mushrooms, and garlic until tender.

3. Transfer sautéed vegetables into large bowl, add chopped artichokes, and remaining ingredients, stirring until combined. Pour mixture into prepared dish. Bake 30 minutes, or until set and top light brown. Cut into squares.

NUTRIENTS

Calories 37

Calories from Fat 28%

Fat 1g

Saturated Fat 1g

Cholesterol 16mg

Sodium 119mg

Carbohydrate 4g

Dietary Fiber 1g

Sugar 1g

Protein 3g

Diabetic Exchanges:
1 vegetable

Artichokes are a naturally low-sodium, fat-free, low calorie food, rich in healthy antioxidants and phytonutrients.

Serve hot, room temperature, or even out of the refrigerator.

BBQ CHICKEN PIZZA

You can easily turn last night's leftover chicken into this amazing restaurant favorite with a store-bought crust and a few simple ingredients.

Makes 8 (1-slice) servings

1 green bell pepper, cored and thinly sliced

1 small red onion, thinly sliced

1 (12-inch) thin pizza crust

3/4 cup barbecue sauce (thicker variety)

1 cup sliced or shredded cooked chicken breasts (Rotisserie chicken)

1 cup shredded part-skim mozzarella cheese

1/2 cup shredded reduced-fat sharp Cheddar cheese

2 tablespoons chopped green onion

1. Preheat oven 425°F.

2. In large nonstick skillet coated with nonstick cooking spray, sauté green pepper and onion until crisp tender.

3. Spread pizza crust with barbecue sauce. Sprinkle evenly with green pepper mixture, chicken, both cheeses and green onion. Bake 8-10 minutes or until light golden brown.

NUTRIENTS

Calories 231

Calories from Fat 25%

Fat 6g

Saturated Fat 3g

Cholesterol 28mg

Sodium 498mg

Carbohydrates 27g

Dietary Fiber 1g

Total Sugars 11g

Protein 15g

Dietary Exchanges:
2 starch, 1 1/2 lean meat

Did you know that by choosing low-fat cheese and dairy products, you are consuming more calcium? This is because the fat in milk doesn't contain calcium, helping with healthy weight management.

CHICKEN THAI PIZZA

 D

Chicken, onion and carrots with peanut sauce make a spunky and robust phenomenal pizza.

Makes 8 (1 slice) servings

1 (12-inch) thin pizza crust
1/4 cup peanut sauce
1 1/2 cups chopped cooked chicken breast
1/2 cup red onion slices
1/2 cup shredded carrots
1/4 cup chopped green onion
1 cup shredded part-skim mozzarella cheese
2 tablespoons chopped fresh cilantro, optional

1. Preheat oven 450°F.
2. Spread pizza crust with peanut sauce. Top with chicken, red onion, carrots, green onion and cheese.
3. Place on oven rack and bake 8-10 minutes or until pizza is lightly browned. Top with cilantro, if desired.

NUTRIENTS

Calories 221
Calories from Fat 31%
Fat 7g
Saturated Fat 2g
Cholesterol 30mg
Sodium 356mg
Carbohydrates 21g
Dietary Fiber 1g
Total Sugars 2g
Protein 16g
Dietary Exchanges:
1 1/2 starch, 2 lean meat

Buy pre-shredded carrots in bag. Purchase chopped green onions in produce department for extra ease.

If Peanut Sauce is too spicy or if desired, substitute barbecue sauce. Can also top with red pepper slices for vitamin C.

SPINACH & ARTICHOKE WHITE PIZZA

A creamy white sauce topped with spinach, artichokes, sun-dried tomatoes, Italian seasoning and cheese turns into a scrumptious pizza.

  D

Makes 8 (1-slice) servings

1 cup skim milk

3 tablespoons all-purpose flour

1/2 teaspoon minced garlic

Salt and pepper to taste

1 (12-inch) thin pizza crust

1 cup coarsely chopped baby spinach

Half small red onion, thinly sliced and halved

1 (14-ounce) can quartered artichokes, drained

3 tablespoons sun-dried tomatoes

1 teaspoon dried basil leaves

1 teaspoon dried oregano leaves

1 cup shredded part-skim mozzarella cheese

1. Preheat oven 425°F.

2. In small nonstick pot, combine milk and flour over medium heat, stirring until thickened. Add garlic and season to taste. Spread white sauce over crust. Top with spinach, onion, artichokes and sun-dried tomatoes. Sprinkle with basil, oregano, and mozzarella cheese.

3. Bake 10 minutes or until crust is golden brown and cheese is melted.

NUTRIENTS

Calories 169

Calories from Fat 23%

Fat 4g

Saturated Fat 2g

Cholesterol 10mg

Sodium 379mg

Carbohydrates 23g

Dietary Fiber 1g

Total Sugars 3g

Protein 10g

Dietary Exchanges:
1 1/2 starch, 1 lean meat

You know spinach is chocked full of nutrition by its vibrant rich green color – concentrated in phytonutrients and flavonoids, offering healthy antioxidant protection.

CHICKEN, RED PEPPER, SPINACH & WHITE BEAN PIZZA

 D

NUTRIENTS

Calories 199

Calories from Fat 28%

Fat 6g

Saturated Fat 2g

Cholesterol 24mg

Sodium 362mg

Carbohydrates 21g

Dietary Fiber 2g

Total Sugars 2g

Protein 14g

Dietary Exchanges:
1 1/2 starch, 1 1/2 lean meat

*Freeze leftover pizza slices
and reheat for a make-
ahead meal another day.
I just took slices out of
the freezer and either I'm
hungry or forgot how good
this pizza was.*

A hearty combination of incredible savory flavors makes this an exceptional pizza.

Makes 8 (1-slice) servings

1 (12-inch) thin pizza crust

2 teaspoons olive oil

1 medium red bell pepper, cored and thinly sliced

1/2 cup chopped red onion

1 teaspoon minced garlic

2 cups chopped baby spinach

1 teaspoon dried oregano leaves

1 cup chopped cooked chicken breast

1/2 cup white navy beans, drained and rinsed

1 cup shredded part-skim mozzarella cheese

1. Preheat oven 425°F. Coat crust with oil.

2. In large nonstick skillet coated with nonstick cooking spray, cook red pepper and onion about 5 minutes or until crisp tender. Add garlic, spinach and oregano, stirring only until spinach is wilted.

3. Evenly spoon spinach mixture over crust and top with remaining ingredients. Bake 8–10 minutes, or until cheese is melted and crust is done.

GREEK CHICKEN BURGERS

An all-American classic goes Greek with this delicious burger.

Makes 4 burgers

 D

1 pound ground chicken

1 egg white

1/3 cup dried bread crumbs

1 teaspoon minced garlic

2 teaspoons dried oregano leaves

1/2 cup coarsely chopped baby spinach leaves

1/4 cup crumbled reduced-fat feta cheese

Salt and pepper to taste

1. Preheat oven 500°F. Line baking pan with foil.
2. In large bowl, combine all ingredients and form into four patties. Place on prepared pan. Cook 15 minutes or until done.

NUTRIENTS

Calories 189

Calories from Fat 22%

Fat 5g

Saturated Fat 2g

Cholesterol 75mg

Sodium 333mg

Carbohydrates 8g

Dietary Fiber 1g

Total Sugars 1g

Protein 28g

Dietary Exchanges:
1/2 starch, 3 lean meat

ASIAN BURGERS

A burger gets an instant flavor-savor Asian makeover.

Makes 4 burgers

D

1/4 cup panko bread crumbs

1/4 cup skim milk

1 pound ground sirloin

1/3 cup chopped green onion

1 tablespoon chopped ginger or 1 teaspoon ground ginger

2 egg whites

1 tablespoon low-sodium soy sauce

2 tablespoons hoisin sauce

1. Preheat oven 500°F. Line baking pan with foil.
2. In large bowl, stir panko bread crumbs and milk; let sit 5 minutes. Add remaining ingredients except hoisin sauce. Form into four patties and place on prepared pan.
3. Cook 15 minutes and brush with hoisin sauce after 10 minutes.

NUTRIENTS

Calories 192

Calories from Fat 27%

Fat 6g

Saturated Fat 2g

Cholesterol 63mg

Sodium 266mg

Carbohydrates 7g

Dietary Fiber 0g

Total Sugars 4g

Protein 27g

Dietary Exchanges:
1/2 starch, 3 lean meat

OPEN FACE BAKED BURGERS

You'll be excited to try this one-step super tasting po-boy style burger.

Makes 8 (heaping 1/3-cup) beef burgers

4 (5-6-inch) small sub rolls, split in half lengthwise

3/4 cup cornflakes, crushed

1 cup chopped onion

1 teaspoon minced garlic

1/3 cup skim milk

5 tablespoons ketchup, divided

1 tablespoon Worcestershire sauce

1/2 teaspoon garlic powder

1 egg white, lightly beaten

Salt and pepper to taste

1 pound ground sirloin

1 cup shredded reduced-fat Cheddar cheese

1. Preheat oven 450°F. Line baking pan with foil.
2. Bake rolls, cut side up, on baking pan until golden and crisp, 4-5 minutes.
3. In bowl, combine cornflakes, onion, garlic, milk, 3 tablespoons ketchup, Worcestershire sauce, garlic powder, egg white and season to taste. Add meat and mix gently until combined.
4. Top toasted rolls evenly with 1/3 cup meat mixture, spreading meat to edges of rolls. Brush tops with remaining ketchup.
5. Bake until meat thermometer registers 160°F 20-25 minutes. Sprinkle with cheese and continue baking until cheese melts, 2-3 minutes.

NUTRIENTS

Calories 229

Calories from Fat 25%

Fat 7g

Saturated Fat 3g

Cholesterol 39mg

Sodium 437mg

Carbohydrates 23g

Dietary Fiber 1g

Total Sugars 6g

Protein 20g

Dietary Exchanges:
1 1/2 starch, 2 1/2 lean meat

Garlic in foods can add more than flavor – as garlic is high in antioxidant content, helping to boost your immune system easing arthritic inflammation.

Top with condiments of your choice.

PHILLY CHEESE STEAK

One of those outrageously delicious and simple sandwiches made with gravy mix and deli meat.

Makes 4 cheese steaks

1 (1-ounce) packet brown gravy mix

1/2 pound shaved deli roast beef

1 small onion, thinly sliced

Half green pepper, cored and thinly sliced

4 buns or rolls

4 slices provolone or Swiss cheese, shredded or thinly sliced

1. In nonstick small pot, prepare gravy mix according to directions. When gravy thickens, add roast beef.

2. Meanwhile, in medium nonstick skillet coated with nonstick cooking spray, sauté onion and green pepper until tender, about 5-7 minutes.

3. Split open rolls and place cheese on one side; toast until cheese is melted. After toasted, place about 1/3 heaping cup meat mixture onto bottom of roll. Top with sliced green pepper and onion and replace other half of roll.

NUTRIENTS

Calories 286

Calories from Fat 30%

Fat 10g

Saturated Fat 4g

Cholesterol 42mg

Sodium 1011mg

Carbohydrates 30g

Dietary Fiber 2g

Total Sugars 5g

Protein 21g

Dietary Exchanges:
2 starch, 2 lean meat, 1/2 fat

TERRIFIC TIP

*Can be served in crock pot
to keep warm.*

STUFFED CHICKEN CAESAR SANDWICH

D

NUTRIENTS

Calories 274

Calories from Fat 13%

Fat 4g

Saturated Fat 1g

Cholesterol 45mg

Sodium 550mg

Carbohydrates 37g

Dietary Fiber 3g

Total Sugars 4g

Protein 24g

Dietary Exchanges:
2 1/2 starch, 2 1/2 lean meat

The Caesar dressing may be used on a salad.

On your next Caesar salad or sandwich, keep the anchovies for a healthy dose of omega-3.

Everyone's favorite salad tossed with rotisserie chicken stuffed into crusty French bread makes a quick-chick sandwich.

Makes 6 sandwiches with (2/3-cup) chicken mixture

1 (16-ounce) loaf French bread or 6 small loaves
 (try whole wheat)

1 large head romaine lettuce, torn into pieces (about 8 cups)

1/4 cup grated Parmesan cheese

2 cups chopped skinless rotisserie chicken breast

1/2 cup nonfat plain yogurt

1/2 teaspoon minced garlic

2 tablespoons lemon juice

1 teaspoon vinegar

1 teaspoon Worcestershire sauce

1 teaspoon Dijon mustard

1. If using large French bread, cut into 6 sections. Hollow out inside and discard extra bread.
2. In large bowl, combine lettuce, cheese, and chicken.
3. In small bowl, whisk together remaining ingredients. Toss with chicken mixture; stuff into each hollow toasted bread section.

CHICKEN LETTUCE WRAPS

Forget the long ingredient list as everything goes into one skillet creating a dynamic chicken lettuce wrap, one of the best you will eat.

Makes 6 (1/2-cup) servings

1 pound ground chicken

1/2 cup chopped onion

1 teaspoon minced garlic

1 tablespoon grated fresh ginger or 1 teaspoon ground ginger

2 tablespoons low-sodium soy sauce

1 tablespoon peanut butter

1 tablespoon honey

2 tablespoons seasoned rice vinegar

1/2 cup chopped green onion

Half (8-ounce) can chopped water chestnuts, drained

1/4 cup chopped peanuts, optional

1 head butter tip or red leaf lettuce

1. In large nonstick skillet, cook ground chicken, onion and garlic until chicken is done. Add ginger.

2. In small microwave-safe bowl, mix soy sauce, peanut butter, honey and vinegar. Microwave 20 seconds, stir. Add to skillet, stirring, until combined. Add green onion and water chestnuts. Sprinkle with peanuts, if desired and serve with lettuce leaves.

NUTRIENTS

Calories 141

Calories from Fat 22%

Fat 3g

Saturated Fat 1g

Cholesterol 48mg

Sodium 301mg

Carbohydrates 10g

Dietary Fiber 2g

Total Sugars 7g

Protein 18g

Dietary Exchanges: 1 vegetable, 1/2 other carbohydrate, 2 1/2 lean meat

Ginger is an immune boosting root, long believed to have medicinal properties – helping with nausea and upset stomach, also having anti-inflammatory benefits.

Ground turkey or ground sirloin may be substituted.

CALZONES

Nothing fancy; this easy-to-make scrumptious recipe gets a thumbs up!

Makes 8 calzones

 D

NUTRIENTS

Calories 190

Calories from Fat 23%

Fat 5g

Saturated Fat 1g

Cholesterol 20mg

Sodium 433mg

Carbohydrates 24g

Dietary Fiber 2g

Total Sugars 5g

Protein 12g

Dietary Exchanges:
1 starch, 1 vegetable, 1 lean meat

Look for "healthy" marinara sauce in the grocery, for a low-sodium, low sugar option.

1/2 pound ground sirloin

1/2 cup chopped onion

1 cup sliced mushrooms

1 teaspoon minced garlic

1 teaspoon dried basil leaves

1/2 teaspoon dried oregano leaves

Salt and pepper to taste

1 (11-ounce) refrigerated roll pizza dough (thin crust)

1/2 cup shredded part-skim mozzarella cheese

1 cup "healthy" marinara sauce

1. Preheat oven 425°F. Coat baking pan with nonstick cooking spray.

2. In large nonstick skillet, cook meat, onion, mushrooms and garlic until meat is done; drain excess fat. Add basil, oregano and season to taste. Set aside.

3. Unroll dough; pat and stretch into rectangle on floured surface. Cut dough into eight squares. Spoon about 1/4 cup beef mixture on each square. Sprinkle evenly with cheese.

4. Fold dough over filling forming into semi-circle mashing edges to form rim. Press fork along edges to seal dough. Prick top of calzones with fork to allow steam to escape. Place on baking pan. Bake 10-12 minutes or until lightly browned. Serve with marinara sauce.

BEEFY CRESCENTS

Nothing beats roast beef, horseradish and cheese in this pastry pick-up.

Makes 8 crescents

1 (8-ounce) package reduced-fat crescent rolls

4 teaspoons Horseradish Sauce or prepared horseradish (found in jar)

1 cup roast beef or 1/2 pound thinly sliced deli roast beef

2 ounces shredded or sliced Jarlsberg cheese (light Swiss)

1. Preheat oven 375°F.
2. Unroll crescents onto large baking pan. Spread about 1/2 teaspoon horseradish on each crescent and top with roast beef and cheese.
3. Roll crescents starting from wide end to narrow end. Bake 11-13 minutes, until crescents are golden.

See page 124 for photo

See page 124 for photo

NUTRIENTS

Calories 147

Calories from Fat 41%

Fat 7g

Saturated Fat 3g

Cholesterol 19mg

Sodium 273mg

Carbohydrates 13g

Dietary Fiber 0g

Total Sugars 3g

Protein 10g

Dietary Exchanges:
1 starch, 1 lean meat, 1/2 fat

HAM & CHEESE SNACK SANDWICHES

Yummy mini ham and Swiss sandwiches.

Makes 24 snack sandwiches

 D

24 miniature rolls

1/3 cup Dijon mustard

2 tablespoons finely chopped onion

Dash hot sauce

1/2 pound thinly sliced lean ham, cut into small pieces

2 cups shredded Jarlsberg cheese (Swiss cheese)

1. Preheat oven 350°F. Line baking pan with foil.
2. Split rolls in half, lay on prepared pan. In small bowl, combine mustard, onion, and hot sauce. Spread each bottom half with mustard mixture and layer ham and cheese. Replace tops.
3. Place filled rolls close together on baking pan and cover with foil. Bake 12-15 minutes or until cheese is melted.

NUTRIENTS

Calories 129

Calories from Fat 27%

Fat 4g

Saturated Fat 1g

Cholesterol 19mg

Sodium 307mg

Carbohydrates 15g

Dietary Fiber 1g

Total Sugars 4g

Protein 8g

Dietary Exchanges:
1 starch, 1 lean meat

Good Morning Cheese Grits (pg 143)

7

TUMMY TROUBLES

Arthritis treatments have made great strides in managing arthritic pain and swelling, as well as slowing the progression of joint damage; however, often the medication comes along with unpleasant side effects. Although, not all arthritis medications may cause the same side effects if any at all, the more frequently noted side effects include an upset stomach and nausea. Each of the symptoms can cause roadblocks when it comes to achieving a healthy nutritious diet. This chapter aims to provide meals, recipes and tips that help combat these common side effects, providing you with tools to eat well while easing your symptoms.

UPSET STOMACH AND NAUSEA:

- When nausea hits, it is best to stay away from the traditional three heavy meals and opt for lighter mini-meals or snacks to get your nutrition.

- Research has also shown that ginger can aid in alleviating nausea and can be soothing to the stomach: gingersnaps, ginger candy, ginger ale.

- Cold and odorless foods help avoid nausea triggers making smoothies just the ticket for a light and easy meal – great for on the go snacking.

- Inexpensive and easy to find, lemons may provide you with instant relief from nausea. Either as an ingredient in a recipe or even just a quick whiff, lemons and citrus foods are a natural way to curb that sick feeling. The smell alone will help as that part of our brain is closely linked with nausea symptoms.

- Prevent triggering nausea by slowing down your liquid intake at mealtime and between meals. Sipping ginger ale or lemon water may help alleviate nausea.

- Rest after meals, without lying down, letting your food settle, and avoiding vigorous activity 30 minutes after a meal.

- Often times, taking medications with food can help reduce nausea symptoms.

- Discuss your symptoms and a plan to reduce them with your doctor.

SOME FOODS TO INCLUDE:

- Dry plain foods such as toast, crackers, pretzels or dry cereal
- Applesauce
- Skinless chicken
- Rice
- Cream of wheat
- Hard candy: peppermint or lemon
- The herb ginger in foods, ginger tea, ginger ale, gingersnaps
- Lemon
- Citrus and fruit smoothies

This chapter aims to provide meals, recipes and tips that help combat these common side effects, providing you with tools to eat well while easing your symptoms.

GINGER TEA

Treat yourself to an invigorating cup of ginger tea with this easy recipe.

Makes 1 serving

4-6 thin slices raw peeled ginger

1 1/2 - 2 cups water

1 tablespoon lemon or lime juice to taste

1-2 tablespoons honey or to taste, optional

1. In small pot, bring ginger and water to boil, lower heat, cover, and simmer at least 10-15 minutes. For stronger and tangier tea, boil 20 minutes or more, and use more slices of ginger.
2. Remove from heat and add lime juice and honey to taste.

NUTRIENTS

Calories 3

Calories from Fat 0%

Fat 0g

Saturated Fat 0g

Cholesterol 0mg

Sodium 11mg

Carbohydrates 1g

Dietary Fiber 0g

Total Sugars 0g

Protein 0g

Dietary Exchanges: Free

APPLESAUCE OATMEAL

A nice alternative to spice up your morning oatmeal.

Makes 2 (3/4-cup) servings

1 cup skim milk

3/4 cup old-fashioned oatmeal

1/2 cup unsweetened applesauce

1 tablespoon light brown sugar

1/8 teaspoon ground cinnamon

1. In small pot, bring milk to boil. Add oatmeal, reduce heat.
2. Cook five minutes or until thickened, stirring occasionally. Add applesauce, brown sugar, and cinnamon stirring until well mixed. Serve immediately.

NUTRIENTS

Calories 212

Calories from Fat 9%

Fat 2g

Saturated Fat 1g

Cholesterol 2mg

Sodium 68mg

Carbohydrate 40g

Dietary Fiber 4g

Total Sugars 19g

Protein 9g

Diabetic Exchanges: 1 1/2 starch, 0.5 fruit, 1/2 skim milk, 1/2 other carbohydrate

SAVORY BREAKFAST BREAD PUDDING

A make-ahead simple, savory cheese soufflé-style dish. Pop in a cold oven if using a glass dish when baking. Remember breakfast type foods are enjoyed and can be served at all times of day.

Makes about 7 (3/4-cup) servings

2 eggs
3 egg whites
1 1/2 cups skim milk
Salt and pepper to taste
Half loaf French or Italian bread, cut into slices, divided
1 1/2 cups shredded reduced-fat Cheddar cheese, divided

1. In mixing bowl beat eggs and egg whites with milk; season to taste. Set aside.
2. Place half of the bread slices in 9x9x2-inch baking dish coated with nonstick cooking spray.
3. Sprinkle with 1 cup cheese. Top with remaining bread and cheese. Pour egg mixture over casserole, refrigerate two hours or overnight.
4. Bake 350°F 30 - 35 minutes or until puffed and golden.

NUTRIENTS

Calories 208
Calories from Fat 28%
Fat 6g
Saturated Fat 3g
Cholesterol 68mg
Sodium 408mg
Carbohydrates 22g
Dietary Fiber 1g
Total Sugars 4g
Protein 15g
Dietary Exchanges:
1 1/2 starch, 2 lean meat

If feeling better, add protein such as chicken, Canadian bacon or ham and can even add spinach or your favorite veggies.

Eggs are the perfect source of protein to boost nutrition when not feeling well.

GOOD MORNING CHEESE GRITS

Grits turn into a satisfying, yet comforting meal with a few extra ingredients.

Makes 4 (1/2-cup) servings

1/3 cup diced Canadian bacon or diced ham
1/2 cup quick grits
2 cups skim milk
1/2 cup low-sodium fat-free chicken broth or skim milk
1/3 cup shredded reduced-fat sharp Cheddar cheese
1/2 teaspoon paprika
Salt and pepper to taste

1. In nonstick pot coated with nonstick cooking spray, cook Canadian bacon until begins to brown. Add grits, milk, and broth. Bring to boil, reduce heat, cover, and continue cooking until grits are done, 5-7 minutes.
2. Stir in cheese and paprika. Season to taste.

NUTRIENTS

Calories 155
Calories from Fat 15%
Fat 2g
Saturated Fat 1g
Cholesterol 14mg
Sodium 272mg
Carbohydrates 22g
Dietary Fiber 0g
Total Sugars 6g
Protein 11g
Dietary Exchanges:
1 starch, 1/2 fat-free milk, 1 lean meat

Adjust ingredients to your taste and how you feel — you may just prefer cheese grits or plain grits.

BANANA PANCAKES

A little extra with bananas makes these pancakes really great!

Makes 10 pancakes

D

1 cup all-purpose flour

1/2 cup whole wheat flour

2 teaspoons baking powder

1/2 teaspoon baking soda

2 ripe bananas, mashed

1 1/4 cups buttermilk

1 egg

1 tablespoon canola oil

1 tablespoon brown sugar

2 bananas, sliced, optional

NUTRIENTS

Calories 124

Calories from Fat 18%

Fat 2g

Saturated Fat 0g

Cholesterol 20mg

Sodium 183mg

Carbohydrates 22g

Dietary Fiber 2g

Total Sugars 6g

Protein 4g

Dietary Exchanges:
1 1/2 starch

1. In large bowl, whisk together both flours, baking powder, and baking soda.

2. In another bowl, whisk together mashed bananas, buttermilk, egg, oil, and brown sugar. Pour into dry ingredients and mix until just combined, do not over mix.

3. Heat skillet or griddle over medium heat with nonstick cooking spray. Pour 1/4 cup batter into skillet and cook until bubbles. Flip and cook other side until golden brown.

4. Serve each pancake with sliced bananas, if desired.

Don't have buttermilk — use 1 cup skim milk plus 1 tablespoon lemon juice or vinegar. Mix and let sit 3 minutes.

Trying using whole-wheat flour or half of each flour to boost nutrition.

OVEN BAKED FRENCH TOAST

Whip up the night before and pop in the oven the next day.

Makes 10 servings

8 ounce loaf French bread (whole wheat may be used),
  cut into 1-inch thick squares

1 (5-ounce) jar seedless all natural blackberry fruit spread

4 ounces reduced-fat cream cheese

2 tablespoons sugar

2 tablespoons skim milk

1 egg

2 egg whites

1/4 cup light brown sugar

1 cup fat-free half-and-half

1 teaspoon vanilla extract

1/2 teaspoon ground cinnamon

1. Coat 9x9x2-inch baking pan with nonstick cooking spray.

2. Place half of French bread squares in prepared baking pan. In microwave-safe dish, heat jam until melted, stirring. Drizzle over bread.

3. In bowl, beat together cream cheese, 2 tablespoons sugar and milk until smooth. Drop over bread mixture and cover with remaining French bread squares.

4. In large bowl, whisk together egg, egg whites, brown sugar, half-and-half, vanilla and cinnamon. Pour mixture evenly over bread. Gently press bread into liquid mixture, cover, and refrigerate as time permits, preferably overnight.

5. Preheat oven 325°F. Bake, covered, 30-35 minutes, uncover 5-10 minutes or until bread is golden.

NUTRIENTS

Calories 184

Calories from Fat 17%

Fat 3g

Saturated Fat 2g

Cholesterol 27mg

Sodium 199mg

Carbohydrates 32g

Dietary Fiber 1g

Total Sugars 17g

Protein 7g

Dietary Exchanges:
1 starch, 1/2 fat-free milk, 1/2 fruit

Substitute your favorite jam flavor if you prefer or leave it out for a plainer version.

GINGERBREAD MUFFINS

   D

Light and fluffy, this muffin has all of the flavor of your favorite spiced cookie in this moist anytime snack or breakfast muffin.

Makes 24 muffins

NUTRIENTS

Calories 134
Calories from Fat 27%
Fat 4g
Saturated Fat 0g
Cholesterol 16mg
Sodium 117mg
Carbohydrates 23g
Dietary Fiber 1g
Total Sugars 12g
Protein 2g
Dietary Exchanges:
1 1/2 starch, 1/2 fat

1 1/2 cups whole wheat flour

1 cup all-purpose flour

1 teaspoon ground ginger

1 teaspoon ground cinnamon

1/2 teaspoon ground cloves

1/2 cup sugar

1/3 cup canola oil

1 cup molasses

2 eggs

1 cup boiling water

2 teaspoons baking soda

1. Preheat oven 325°F. Line muffin tins with paper liners or nonstick cooking spray.

2. In large bowl, combine both flours, ginger, cinnamon, and cloves. Set aside.

3. In medium bowl, whisk together sugar and oil. Add molasses and eggs whisking until blended. In glass measuring cup, combine water and baking soda; stir to dissolve. Pour in egg mixture and whisk until blended. Add egg mixture into flour mixture, stirring just until combined.

4. Spoon batter into paper lined tins, filling 1/2-3/4 full. Bake 20-25 minutes or until inserted toothpick comes out clean.

Keep some muffins in the freezer to pop out when not feeling well and need a boost.

Ginger has been shown to help nausea symptoms so these muffins may be just the ticket to feeling better.

BANANA MUFFINS

A mild easy-to-make basic but exceptionally tasty banana muffin.

Makes 18 muffins

   D

4 ounces reduced-fat cream cheese

3/4 cup light brown sugar

1 1/2 cups mashed bananas (3 bananas)

2 egg whites

1 teaspoon vanilla extract

1 3/4 cups biscuit baking mix

1. Preheat oven 400°F. Line muffin tins with paper liners or nonstick cooking spray.
2. In mixing bowl, cream together cream cheese and brown sugar. Beat in bananas, egg whites, and vanilla.
3. Stir in biscuit mix just until blended. Spoon batter into paper lined tins, filling 1/2-3/4 full. Bake 15-20 minutes or until golden brown.

NUTRIENTS

Calories 117

Calories from Fat 22%

Fat 3g

Saturated Fat 1g

Cholesterol 5mg

Sodium 174mg

Carbohydrates 21g

Dietary Fiber 1g

Total Sugars 12g

Protein 2g

Dietary Exchanges:
1 1/2 starch, 1/2 fat

When feeling better, add chocolate chips, pecans, cranberries or your favorite addition to spruce up the muffin.

I like to have muffins as they may be kept in the freezer to eat whenever you have a craving.

CHICKEN & DUMPLINGS

Ready in no time at all, this ultimate comfort food and soothing soup is made with rotisserie chicken and drop dumplings.

Makes 8 (1-cup) servings

1 onion, chopped

1 cup baby carrots

1/2 teaspoon minced garlic

3 tablespoons all-purpose flour

6 cups low-sodium fat-free chicken broth, divided

1/2 teaspoon dried thyme leaves

2 cups chopped skinless rotisserie chicken breast

2 cups biscuit baking mix

2/3 cup skim milk

Salt and pepper to taste

1. In large nonstick pot coated with nonstick cooking spray, sauté onion, carrots, and garlic over medium heat until tender.
2. In small cup, stir flour with 1/3 cup chicken broth, mixing until smooth. Gradually add flour mixture and remaining broth to pot; bring to boil. Add thyme and chicken and bring to boil.
3. In bowl, stir together biscuit baking mix and milk. Drop mixture by spoonfuls into boiling broth.
4. Return to boil, reduce heat, and cook, covered, carefully stirring occasionally, 15-20 minutes or until dumplings are done. Season to taste. If soup is too thick, add more broth.

NUTRIENTS

Calories 212

Calories from Fat 22%

Fat 5g

Saturated Fat 1g

Cholesterol 32mg

Sodium 553mg

Carbohydrates 26g

Dietary Fiber 2g

Total Sugars 4g

Protein 15g

Dietary Exchanges:
1 1/2 starch, 1 vegetable, 1 1/2 lean meat

A short-cut for dumplings: cut flaky biscuits into fourths and drop into boiling broth or you can even use flour tortillas cut into fourths. You can slice carrots — but I find baby carrots a time-saver.

Avoid vigorous activity 30 minutes after meals to let food settle and avoid upsetting your stomach.

SIMPLE BAKED CHICKEN

Such tender chicken with gravy tastes like chicken soup. Be sure to serve with rice to soak in the last drop of gravy.

Makes 6 servings

 D

1 1/2 pounds chicken breast tenders
1/4 cup biscuit baking mix
1 tablespoon olive oil
1 teaspoon minced garlic
1 tablespoon all-purpose flour
1 (16-ounce) can low-sodium fat-free chicken broth

1. Preheat oven 375°F. Coat 3-quart oblong baking dish with nonstick cooking spray.
2. Coat chicken in baking mix and place in prepared dish. Bake 40 minutes.
3. In small nonstick pot, combine oil and garlic, and add flour. Whisk in chicken broth, bring to boil, and cook until slightly thickened. Pour over chicken, and continue baking, covered with foil, another 20-30 minutes, or until chicken is done.

NUTRIENTS
Calories 173
Calories from Fat 30%
Fat 6g
Saturated Fat 1g
Cholesterol 73mg
Sodium 197mg
Carbohydrates 3g
Dietary Fiber 0g
Total Sugars 0g
Protein 25g
Dietary Exchanges:
3 lean meat

When not feeling well, simple, protein-rich foods such as this can help keep up your nutrition when not in the mood for anything else.

BAKED CHICKEN SCAMPI

You'll love the flavor of this simple, moist chicken with a light Italian-like scampi seasoning.

Makes 6 servings

1 1/2 pounds boneless, skinless chicken breasts

1 tablespoon olive oil

2 tablespoons grated Parmesan cheese

1 tablespoon dried parsley flakes

1/4 teaspoon garlic powder

Salt and pepper to taste

2 teaspoons dried oregano leaves

3 tablespoons lemon juice

2 tablespoons Worcestershire sauce

1. Combine all ingredients in shallow bowl. Marinate, covered, in refrigerator several hours or overnight.

2. Preheat broiler. Remove chicken from marinade and place in single layer in shallow baking dish or broiling pan. Broil 8 inches from heat, turning once, until chicken is done, about another 15 minutes.

NUTRIENTS

Calories 166

Calories from Fat 32%

Fat 6g

Saturated Fat 1g

Cholesterol 74mg

Sodium 214mg

Carbohydrates 2g

Dietary Fiber 0g

Total Sugars 1g

Protein 25g

Dietary Exchanges:
3 lean meat

You will find this dish to be light and easy on your gastrointestinal tract.

Boiled plain pasta and dry toast is a good meal to try when you first start to feel better.

QUICK CHICKEN PASTA

A quick comforting chicken and pasta pairing. If you can't tolerate mushrooms, onion or tomato, leave out for simpler version, until you feel better.

 D

Makes 6 (1 1/3-cup) servings

1 tablespoon olive oil

1 1/2 pounds boneless skinless chicken breasts, cut into strips

Salt and pepper to taste

1 teaspoon minced garlic

1 tablespoon dried basil leaves

1 large tomato, diced, optional

1 cup sliced mushrooms, optional

1/2 cup chopped red onion, optional

1/3 cup low-sodium fat-free chicken broth

1 (8-ounce) package angel hair pasta

1. In large pan coated with nonstick cooking spray, heat oil and sauté chicken until almost done, about 4 minutes. Season to taste.

2. Add garlic and basil; and tomato, mushrooms, and onion, if desired, stirring 5 minutes or until veggies are tender. Add chicken broth, cooking until heated through.

3. Meanwhile, cook pasta according to package directions; drain. When chicken is done, toss with pasta.

NUTRIENTS

Calories 293

Calories from Fat 12%

Fat 6g

Saturated Fat 1g

Cholesterol 73mg

Sodium 138mg

Carbohydrates 29g

Dietary Fiber 1g

Total Sugars 1g

Protein 29g

Dietary Exchanges:
2 starch, 3 lean meat

NUTRITIONAL **NUGGET**

By slowing down your liquid intake at meal time and between meals, you may help prevent triggering nausea.

LIGHT & LEMON ANGEL HAIR

 D

Sometimes a tart citrus taste is soothing to the stomach. This light pasta goes easily with whatever you're serving or alone for a comfort pasta dish.

Makes 4 servings

8 ounces angel hair pasta

1/2 teaspoon minced garlic

2 tablespoons olive oil

3 tablespoons lemon juice

1 1/2 teaspoons grated lemon rind, optional

1/3 cup chopped parsley

Salt and pepper to taste

1. Cook pasta according to package directions, reserving 1/4 cup cooking water; drain well and set aside. Transfer pasta to large serving dish.

2. Add remaining ingredients including reserved 1/4 cup cooking water; toss together until well combined. Serve warm or at room temperature.

NUTRIENTS

Calories 276

Calories from Fat 25%

Fat 8g

Saturated Fat 1g

Cholesterol 0mg

Sodium 9mg

Carbohydrates 44g

Dietary Fiber 2g

Total Sugars 2g

Protein 8g

Dietary Exchanges:
3 starch, 1 fat

If making pasta ahead of time, drizzle and toss with a little olive oil to prevent from sticking together.

Even if just a quick sniff, lemons may provide instant relief for nausea symptoms.

RICE PUDDING

A mild, creamy tapioca pudding –type recipe that could be used as a morning meal or light dessert. When you have extra rice, here's a good option.

Makes 4 (1/2-cup) servings

1 1/2 cups cooked white rice
2 cups skim milk, divided
1/4 cup sugar
Dash salt
1 egg, beaten
1 teaspoon vanilla extract

1. In medium nonstick pot, combine cooked rice, 1 1/2 cups milk, sugar and salt. Cook over medium heat, stirring, until thick and creamy, 10-15 minutes.

2. In bowl, combine remaining 1/2 cup milk and egg. Gradually pour some of the hot mixture, stirring, into milk-egg mixture. Return to pot. Bring to boil, stirring constantly, and cook until thickened, several minutes. Remove from heat and add vanilla.

NUTRIENTS

Calories 188
Calories from Fat 7%
Fat 1g
Saturated Fat 1g
Cholesterol 49mg
Sodium 70mg
Carbohydrates 36g
Dietary Fiber 0g
Total Sugars 19g
Protein 7g
Dietary Exchanges: 1 starch, 1/2 fat-free milk, 1 other carbohydrate

TERRIFIC TIP

To reheat, stir in milk until creamy consistency — can reheat in microwave. The mixture thickens as it cools.

NUTRITIONAL NUGGET

Ounce per ounce, low fat milk and dairy contain more calcium than the full-fat version because the fat replaces the calcium.

Lemon Feta Chicken (pg 164)

8

FIGHT FATIGUE

When dealing with arthritis, fatigue can be a common symptom, disrupting your quality of life and hindering your ability to receive good nutrition. Fatigue can be difficult to pinpoint the problem, however there are several reasons you may be experiencing fatigue in conjunction with arthritis. Discuss with your doctor possible sources of the problem, therefore allowing you and your care team to develop a treatment plan.

POSSIBLE FATIGUE CAUSES:

INFLAMMATION - Cytokines are released by the body that cause inflammation in psoriatic or other kinds of inflammatory arthritis; anti-inflammatory pain relievers may alleviate some of this cause of fatigue.

ANEMIA – Anemia can present with arthritis, when the body does not have enough healthy red blood cells, which are used by the body to carry oxygen to the blood tissues. When this process does not work properly, fatigue ensues, so be sure to rule out anemia as this underlying cause can be treated.

DEPRESSION - Common with chronic illness, depression can present itself as fatigue or worsen existing fatigue. Seek community support by connecting with others in similar situations, and discuss treatment options, whether medicinal or therapy, with your doctor.

EXERCISE – Although you may not feel well enough to be active, inactivity from painful arthritis can actually make you feel more tired. Exercise can give you more energy, but don't overdo it as 30 minutes of moderate exercise most days is adequate. Exercise also helps to maintain a healthy weight, which is also important to reduce arthritic pain.

MEDICATION – Arthritis medication can negatively impact your energy level. Discuss possible medication timing changes with your doctor.

Adjust your schedule as necessary to allow for enough rest time, including naps that can help restore your energy.

Take advantage of time when you are feeling well to prepare ahead of time, such as laying out clothes or packing a lunch for the next day.

Make sure you get a good nights sleep by avoiding heavy meals, caffeine and alcohol before bedtime and ensuring your bedroom is dark, quiet and peaceful.

Eating right and good nutrition is necessary to limit fatigue and maximize energy.

Maximize your energy by eating a balanced diet, of complex carbohydrates, protein, and unsaturated fats. Try not to skip meals as good nutrition is fuel keeping your fatigue at bay and your energy up throughout the day.

ENERGY PROVIDING MACRONUTRIENTS:

CARBOHYDRATES – The body's main source of fuel, carbohydrates are the macronutrient that we need in the largest amount and also are easily used by the body as energy. Choosing complex carbohydrates, such as nutritious oats, whole grains, provides the body with fiber and nutrients helping maintain healthy weight and optimize energy.

COMPLEX CARBOHYDRATE FOOD CHOICES:
- Whole Grains: barley, oatmeal, brown rice, whole grain pasta
- Fruits and Vegetables
- Beans and Legumes
- Skim Milk

PROTEIN - Protein helps to ensure growth, to repair body tissue, and to maintain a healthy immune system. Without enough protein, the body can take longer to recover from illness and you can have a lower resistance to infection.

LEAN PROTEIN FOOD CHOICES:
- Eggs
- Lean meat, fish, and poultry
- Low fat dairy products
- Nuts
- Beans, peas, lentils
- Soy foods

FAT – Although fats are the most concentrated source of calories, which too much of can lead to weight gain, they are also essential in normal growth and development. Healthy unsaturated fats help your body to absorb and use vitamins, as well as helping to maintain cell membranes.

UNSATURATED FAT FOOD CHOICES:
- Oils: olive, canola, grapeseed, safflower, walnut, avocado
- Nuts: almonds, cashews, pecans, peanut butter, walnuts
- Avocado
- Fish: salmon, tuna
- Flaxseed
- Sesame seeds

HARVEST GRANOLA

Fantastic and versatile-you are in for a granola treat chocked full of my favorite fall ingredients. Yum, yum, yum!

Makes 20 (1/3-cup) servings

2 tablespoons butter

1/4 cup mashed cooked sweet potatoes

2 tablespoons molasses

1/3 cup maple syrup

4 cups old-fashioned oatmeal

1/3 cup pumpkin seeds

1/2 cup dried cranberries

1/4 cup coarsely chopped pecans

1/3 cup coarsely chopped walnuts

1 teaspoon ground cinnamon

1/4 teaspoon ground cloves

Hearty dash salt

1. Preheat oven 300°F. Line baking pan with foil and coat with nonstick cooking spray.

2. In microwave-safe cup or dish, combine butter, sweet potatoes, molasses and maple syrup. Microwave about 3 minutes or until very bubbly.

3. In large bowl, combine remaining ingredients. Pour butter mixture over oatmeal mixture, tossing until well mixed. Transfer to prepared pan and bake 35-40 minutes, stirring mixture about half way through. Cool.

NUTRIENTS

Calories 132

Calories from Fat 34%

Fat 5g

Saturated Fat 1g

Cholesterol 3mg

Sodium 12mg

Carbohydrates 19g

Dietary Fiber 3g

Total Sugars 7g

Protein 3g

Dietary Exchanges: 1 starch, 1 fat

TERRIFIC TIP

Great for breakfast, snack and to top yogurt. Jarred in mason jars makes a great homemade gift.

You can use canned or cooked leftover sweet potatoes.

OATMEAL BLUEBERRY BREAKFAST BAKE

❄ 🥕 G D

NUTRIENTS

Calories 162

Calories from Fat 19%

Fat 4g

Saturated Fat 1g

Cholesterol 25mg

Sodium 87mg

Carbohydrates 28g

Dietary Fiber 3g

Total Sugars 13g

Protein 5g

Dietary Exchanges: 2 starch, 1/2 fat

NUTRITIONAL NUGGET

Oats are an excellent source of soluble fiber, which helps keep you feel full longer as well as stabilizing blood sugar.

Start your day off right with this moist quick blueberry oatmeal bake. Keep in the refrigerator to enjoy all week.

Makes 9 servings

2 1/2 cups old-fashioned oatmeal

1 teaspoon baking powder

1 teaspoon ground cinnamon

1 tablespoon butter, melted

2 cups skim milk

1/3 cup sugar

1 egg

1 teaspoon vanilla extract

1 cup blueberries, fresh or frozen (more if desired)

1. Preheat oven 375°F. Coat 9x9x2-inch baking pan with nonstick cooking spray.

2. In bowl, combine oatmeal, baking powder, and cinnamon. In small bowl, whisk together butter, milk, sugar, egg and vanilla; set aside.

3. Spoon half oatmeal mixture into prepared baking dish, and half the blueberries. Top with remaining oatmeal mixture and sprinkle with remaining blueberries on top, pressing them in slightly. Pour milk mixture, evenly over.

4. Bake 30-35 minutes, or until light golden brown along the edges, and center is set.

MILDLY MEXICAN BREAKFAST BAKE

This overnight sensation with bright colors and bold flavors will wake up those morning taste-buds!

Makes 8 (1-cup) servings

8 ounces ground breakfast turkey sausage

1 onion, chopped

1 red, green, or yellow bell pepper, cored and chopped

2 cups baby spinach

1 teaspoon minced garlic

1 (4-ounce) can chopped green chilies

4 eggs

6 egg whites

2 cups fat-free half-and-half

2 teaspoons chili powder

1/2 teaspoon ground cumin

1 1/2 cups reduced-fat shredded Mexican blend cheese

5 (8-inch) 98% fat-free flour tortillas, cut into quarters (use corn for Gluten-free option)

1/2 cup chopped green onion

1. Coat 13x9x2-inch baking dish with nonstick cooking spray.

2. In large nonstick skillet, cook and crumble sausage until starts to brown. Add onion and bell pepper, cooking until sausage is done and vegetables tender. Add spinach, garlic and green chilies; cooking until spinach wilts, about 2 minutes.

3. In large bowl, whisk together eggs, egg whites, half-and-half, chili powder, cumin and cheese.

4. Spoon one-third of sausage mixture in baking dish. Top with one-third tortilla quarters and one-third cheese and green onion. Repeat layers, ending with green onion. Pour egg mixture evenly over casserole and refrigerate, covered, at least 6 hours or overnight.

5. Preheat oven 350°F. If using glass baking dish, place in cold oven and bake 50-60 minutes or until bubbly, golden brown and knife inserted into custard comes out clean.

See page 8 for photo

NUTRIENTS

Calories 309

Calories from Fat 35%

Fat 12g

Saturated Fat 4g

Cholesterol 151mg

Sodium 751mg

Carbohydrates 29g

Dietary Fiber 3g

Total Sugars 7g

Protein 23g

Dietary Exchanges: 1 starch, 1/2 fat-free milk, 1 vegetable

Be sure to look for omega-3 fortified eggs, for extra anti-inflammatory benefits.

EGG SALAD WITH EXTRA

NUTRIENTS

Calories 136

Calories from Fat 22%

Fat 3g

Saturated Fat 1g

Cholesterol 62mg

Sodium 464mg

Carbohydrates 16g

Dietary Fiber 4g

Total Sugars 2g

Protein 11g

Dietary Exchanges: 1
starch, 1 lean meat

Protein packed with flavor to match, a versatile egg salad.

Makes 6 (1/2-cup) servings

4 hard-boiled eggs, whites only, chopped

2 hard-boiled eggs, chopped

1 (15-ounce) can small white beans, rinsed and drained

3 tablespoons chopped Kalamata olives

1/4 cup chopped green onion

1 1/2 teaspoons Dijon mustard

3 tablespoons Greek nonfat plain yogurt

Salt and pepper to taste

1. In bowl, mix together all ingredients until well combined.

NUTRITIONAL NUGGET

Eggs are known as the "Perfect Protein" since they have the highest biological value — a measure of how well it supports your body's protein needs — of any food.

TERRIFIC TIP

I hate opening a can of beans and having some left so I used the whole can. Adjust the beans to your preference.

GREEK TUNA SALAD

Add rich and healthy Mediterranean ingredients for a terrific tuna salad.

Makes 8 (1/2-cup) servings

10 ounces canned albacore tuna, drained

1 (14-ounce) can quartered artichokes, drained

2 tablespoons coarsely chopped Kalamata olives

1/2 cup chopped Roma tomatoes

1/2 cup chopped red onion

1/3 cup chopped red or green bell pepper

1 tablespoon lemon juice

1/2 cup Greek nonfat plain yogurt

3-4 fresh basil leaves, torn or 1 teaspoon dried basil leaves

1/4 cup chopped parsley (prefer fresh)

1 teaspoon dried oregano leaves

Salt and pepper to taste

1. In large bowl, combine tuna, artichokes, olives, tomatoes, red onion, and bell pepper. Add remaining ingredients, mixing carefully. Season to taste.

G D

NUTRIENTS

Calories 76

Calories from Fat 12%

Fat 1g

Saturated Fat 0g

Cholesterol 11mg

Sodium 256mg

Carbohydrates 5g

Dietary Fiber 1g

Total Sugars 2g

Protein 11g

Dietary Exchanges: 1 vegetable, 1 1/2 lean meat

TERRIFIC TIP

When a recipe calls for more than several tablespoons parsley, fresh is best, but dried may be used.

NUTRITIONAL NUGGET

Did you know parsley is a good source of plant iron?

WONDERFUL WHITE CHILI

A satisfying bowl of chili with minimal preparation and maximum taste.

Makes 8 (1-cup) servings

1 pound ground chicken

1 onion, chopped

1 teaspoon minced garlic

1 (16-ounce) can white navy beans, rinsed and drained

1 (14 1/2-ounce) can low-sodium fat-free chicken broth

1 (4-ounce) can chopped green chiles

2 cups frozen corn

1 teaspoon ground cumin

2 teaspoons chili powder

1. In large nonstick pot, cook chicken, onion, and garlic until chicken is done. Add remaining ingredients and bring to boil. Reduce heat and cook, covered 15 minutes, until heated.

NUTRIENTS

Calories 183

Calories from Fat 11%

Fat 2g

Saturated Fat 0g

Cholesterol 36mg

Sodium 378mg

Carbohydrates 24g

Dietary Fiber 5g

Total Sugars 4g

Protein 18g

Dietary Exchanges: 1 1/2 starch, 2 lean meat

TEX MEX RICE

Open cans for this yummy meatless entrée or hearty family-pleasing side.

Makes 12 (2/3-cup) servings

2 cups cooked yellow rice

1 (15-ounce) can corn, drained

1 (15-ounce) can black beans, rinsed and drained

1 (10-ounce) can chopped tomatoes and green chilies

1 (2 1/4-ounce) can sliced black olives, drained

1 cup nonfat sour cream

2 cups shredded reduced-fat Mexican blend cheese, divided

1 bunch green onions, chopped (reserving 2 tablespoons)

1. Preheat oven 350°F. Coat 2-quart oblong baking dish with nonstick cooking spray.

2. Combine all ingredients using 1 3/4 cups cheese in prepared dish. Bake 45-50 minutes. Remove from oven and sprinkle with remaining 1/4 cup cheese and 2 tablespoons green onion. Return to oven 5 minutes or until cheese is melted.

NUTRIENTS

Calories 176

Calories from Fat 25%

Fat 5g

Saturated Fat 2g

Cholesterol 15mg

Sodium 618mg

Carbohydrates 22g

Dietary Fiber 4g

Total Sugars 4g

Protein 9g

Dietary Exchanges: 1 1/2 starch, 1 lean meat

CRUNCHY COCONUT CHICKEN FINGERS

Delicious and crunchy, this combination turns chicken fingers into a true specialty.

 D

Makes 4 servings

1 pound boneless, skinless chicken breasts,
   cut into 3 1/2 inch strips

Salt and pepper to taste

1/3 cup lite coconut milk

1 egg white

1/2 teaspoon chili garlic sauce, optional

1/3 cup coconut flakes

3/4 cup cornflake crumbs

1/4 cup sliced almonds

1. Preheat oven 400°F. Line baking pan with foil and coat with nonstick cooking spray.

2. Season chicken to taste. In shallow bowl, whisk together coconut milk, egg white, and chili garlic sauce, if desired. Add chicken.

3. In food processor, pulse together coconut, cornflake crumbs and almonds until finely chopped. Transfer to large plate.

4. Remove chicken strips from coconut milk mixture, letting excess drip back into bowl and coat evenly with cornflake mixture. Place coated chicken on prepared pan. Bake 20-25 minutes; turning chicken halfway though, cooking until chicken is golden and tender.

NUTRIENTS

Calories 230

Calories from Fat 28%

Fat 7g

Saturated Fat 2g

Cholesterol 73mg

Sodium 246mg

Carbohydrates 15g

Dietary Fiber 1g

Total Sugars 3g

Protein 26g

Dietary Exchanges: 1 starch, 3 lean meat

Place cornflakes into food processor to make into crumbs.

Serve with sweetened chili sauce for an Asian touch, fruit salsa or plain.

This protein-rich carb-combo gives a well balanced meal to fuel your energy.

LEMON FETA CHICKEN

G D

A few ingredients transform chicken into a delightful and memorable recipe.

Makes 8 servings

NUTRIENTS

Calories 156

Calories from Fat 26%

Fat 4g

Saturated Fat 2g

Cholesterol 76mg

Sodium 280mg

Carbohydrates 1g

Dietary Fiber 0g

Total Sugars 0g

Protein 26g

Dietary Exchanges: 3 1/2 lean meat

2 pounds boneless, skinless, chicken breasts

1/4 cup lemon juice, divided

1 tablespoon dried oregano leaves, divided

Pepper to taste

3 ounces crumbled reduced-fat feta cheese

3 tablespoons chopped green onion

1. Preheat oven 350°F. Coat 13x9x2-inch baking pan with nonstick cooking spray.

2. Place chicken in prepared baking dish, drizzle with half the lemon juice. Sprinkle with half the oregano and pepper. Top with cheese and green onion. Drizzle with remaining lemon juice and oregano.

3. Bake, covered, 45 minutes-1 hour, or until done.

NUTRITIONAL
NUGGET

Citrus, such as lemons, are high in the antioxidant Vitamin C, important for collagen formation, tissue repair and reduced inflammation.

CHICKEN DIVAN

Chicken and broccoli create an easy comfort-style one-dish meal.

Makes 6 servings

1 1/2 pounds boneless, skinless chicken breast tenders
Salt and pepper to taste
2 (10-ounce) packages frozen chopped broccoli
1/4 cup all-purpose flour
2 cups skim milk
1/3 cup Italian or plain bread crumbs
1 cup shredded reduced-fat sharp Cheddar cheese

1. Preheat oven 350°F. Coat 2-quart oblong baking dish with nonstick cooking spray.

2. Season chicken to taste. In nonstick skillet coated with nonstick cooking spray, cook chicken over medium heat, 10 minutes or until done and lightly browned. Cut into chunks.

3. Meanwhile, cook broccoli according to package directions. Drain and place along bottom of prepared pan. Top with cooked chicken.

4. In nonstick pot, combine flour and milk, cook over medium heat, stirring, until thickened. Remove from heat. Pour sauce evenly over chicken. Sprinkle with bread crumbs and cheese. Bake 20-30 minutes or until mixture is bubbly and heated.

NUTRIENTS

Calories 279

Calories from fat 22%

Fat 7g

Saturated Fat 3g

Cholesterol 84mg

Sodium 406mg

Carbohydrate 17g

Dietary Fiber 3g

Total Sugars 6g

Protein 36g

Diabetic Exchanges: 1 starch, 1 vegetable, 4 1/2 lean meat

Save a step with leftover cooked chicken or Rotisserie chicken.

Fresh broccoli florets may be used instead of frozen chopped broccoli.

CHICKEN & ARTICHOKE LASAGNA

Creamy lasagna is extra easy with Rotisserie chicken and no boil pasta!

Makes 8-10 servings

NUTRIENTS

Calories 297

Calories from Fat 32%

Fat 11g

Saturated Fat 5g

Cholesterol 67mg

Sodium 439mg

Carbohydrates 25g

Dietary Fiber 2g

Total Sugars 5g

Protein 25g

Dietary Exchanges: 1 1/2 starch, 1 vegetable, 3 lean meat

Make your own "TV dinners" by freezing individual portions of lasagna to pull out for a quick-fix meal. Wrap in plastic wrap and store in zip-top freezer plastic bags.

3 cups shredded cooked chicken breast (Rotisserie chicken)

1 (14-ounce) can artichoke hearts, drained and chopped

1/2 cup chopped or julienne cut sun-dried tomatoes

1 cup baby spinach

2 teaspoons dried basil leaves

2 1/2 cups skim milk

1/2 teaspoon garlic powder

2 tablespoons all-purpose flour

1 (8-ounce) package reduced-fat cream cheese

1 1/2 cups shredded part-skim mozzarella cheese

1 (8-ounce) package no-boil lasagna noodles

1. Preheat oven 350°F. Coat 13x9x2-inch baking pan with nonstick cooking spray.

2. In bowl, mix chicken, artichokes, tomatoes, spinach, and basil.

3. In medium nonstick pot, whisk together milk, garlic powder and flour; cook over medium heat, stirring constantly, until comes to boil. Boil several minutes, stirring, or until thickened. Add cream cheese, stirring until melted. Add 1 1/3 cups cream cheese sauce to chicken mixture; set aside.

4. Spread thin layer of remaining cream cheese sauce on bottom of prepared pan. Cover with layer of noodles and half chicken mixture, one-third of mozzarella and one-third cream cheese sauce. Repeat layers of noodles, chicken mixture, mozzarella and sauce. Top with remaining noodles, cream cheese sauce and mozzarella. Bake, covered, 45-50 minutes or until noodles tender.

ITALIAN CHICKEN PASTA

Don't let the ingredient list fool you, as this hearty Italian flavored chicken stir-fry is quick to whip up.

Makes 8 (1-cup) servings

 D

1 (12-ounce) package linguine or thicker spaghetti

1 3/4 pounds boneless, skinless chicken breasts, cut into strips

1/4 cup olive oil

1 teaspoon minced garlic

1 onion, chopped

1/2 pound sliced fresh mushrooms

1 red or green bell pepper, cored and chopped

1 teaspoon dried oregano leaves

1 teaspoon dried basil leaves

1/2 teaspoon thyme leaves

Salt and pepper to taste

1/4 cup grated Parmesan cheese, optional

1. Cook linguine according to package directions; drain. Set aside.
2. In large nonstick skillet, cook chicken in oil over medium high heat, stirring until lightly brown and done, 7 minutes.
3. Add garlic, onion, mushrooms, red pepper, oregano, basil, thyme, and season to taste sautéing until tender. Add pasta tossing to combine. Sprinkle with Parmesan cheese, if desired.

NUTRIENTS

Calories 349

Calories from Fat 27%

Fat 10g

Saturated Fat 2g

Cholesterol 64mg

Sodium 121mg

Carbohydrates 35g

Dietary Fiber 2g

Total Sugars 4g

Protein 28g

Dietary Exchanges: 2 starch, 1 vegetable, 3 lean meat

Look for pre-chopped onion in the produce section of grocery for extra ease.

TERRIFIC THAI SHRIMP

 D

A simple shrimp and pasta dish with an alluring mild sauce of garlic, ginger, peanut butter, and peanuts.

Makes 4 servings

NUTRIENTS

Calories 384

Calories from Fat 22%

Fat 9g

Saturated Fat 1g

Cholesterol 143mg

Sodium 407mg

Carbohydrates 48g

Dietary Fiber 3g

Total Sugars 4g

Protein 26g

Dietary Exchanges: 3 starch, 2 1/2 lean meat

Both garlic and ginger have anti-inflammatory benefits.

1 1/2 cups low-sodium fat-free chicken broth

1 tablespoon low-sodium soy sauce

1 tablespoon plus 1 teaspoon peanut butter

2 teaspoons sesame oil

1 green bell pepper, cored and chopped

1 teaspoon minced garlic

1 tablespoon minced fresh ginger or 1 teaspoon ground ginger

1 pound medium shrimp, peeled

1 (8-ounce) package vermicelli

2 tablespoons dry roasted chopped peanuts

1/4 cup chopped green onion

1. In microwave-safe dish, mix together broth, soy sauce, peanut butter, and sesame oil. Whisk until blended: set aside.

2. In large nonstick skillet coated with nonstick cooking spray, sauté green pepper, garlic and ginger over medium heat 3 minutes. Add shrimp, cook several minutes. Add broth mixture to shrimp, continue cooking until shrimp are done, 3-5 minutes.

3. Cook pasta according to package directions. Drain; toss with shrimp mixture. Sprinkle with peanuts and green onion.

SHRIMP ORZO BAKE

Scrumptious shrimp and a few fresh ingredients make a quick one-dish dinner.

Makes 4 (1-cup) servings

1 cup chopped onion

1 tablespoon minced garlic

2 cups grape or cherry tomato halves

Salt and pepper to taste

12 ounces orzo

3 1/2 cups low-sodium fat-free chicken broth

1 pound peeled medium large shrimp

2 teaspoons olive oil

1/3 cup chopped fresh basil leaves or
   1 tablespoon dried basil leaves

1. Preheat oven 400°F. with rack in top position. Coat 2-quart baking dish with nonstick cooking spray.

2. In large nonstick skillet, cook onion, garlic and tomatoes until tomatoes softened, 5-7 minutes. Season to taste.

3. Add orzo, broth, and sautéed ingredients to baking dish. Cover with foil and bake about 30 minutes or until liquid is almost absorbed.

4. Turn oven to broil. Season shrimp to taste and place shrimp on top of orzo. Drizzle with olive oil. Broil until shrimp are done, 5-7 minutes or opaque in color. Sprinkle with basil.

NUTRIENTS

Calories 469

Calories from Fat 10%

Fat 5g

Saturated Fat 1g

Cholesterol 143mg

Sodium 325mg

Carbohydrates 74g

Dietary Fiber 4g

Total Sugars 8g

Protein 30g

Dietary Exchanges: 4 1/2 starch, 2 vegetable, 2 1/2 lean meat

Shrimp are high in selenium, while low selenium may also be linked to rheumatoid arthritis. The mineral helps antioxidants fight free radicals, regulate the thyroid gland and may prevent cancer.

Orzo is a rice shaped pasta.

BLACKENED FISH

One of my favorite fish recipes — quick, no-fuss, and wonderful. If you don't cook fish, here's the recipe to try.

Makes 4 servings

NUTRIENTS

Calories 232
Calories from Fat 36%
Fat 9g
Saturated Fat 1g
Cholesterol 63mg
Sodium 395mg
Carbohydrates 3g
Dietary Fiber 2g
Total Sugars 0g
Protein 34g
Dietary Exchanges: 4 1/2 lean meat

2 tablespoons paprika
1 teaspoon chili powder
1/2 teaspoon dried thyme leaves
1 teaspoon garlic powder
1 teaspoon pepper
1/2 teaspoon salt
1 1/2 pounds fish fillets
2 tablespoons olive oil

1. In small bowl or plastic bag, combine all ingredients, except fish and oil. Coat both sides of fish with seasoning mixture.

2. In large nonstick skillet, heat oil over medium-high heat. Place fish in hot pan and cook 2-3 minutes on each side until fish flakes with fork.

Fish is done when center is white and opaque — no longer translucent. Any fresh fish may be used such as grouper, halibut, tilapia, trout or catfish.

When available, choose mackerel or rainbow trout for their high omega-3 fatty acid content, helping reduce joint pain inflammation and risk for heart disease.

CRISPY SOUTHWESTERN LASAGNA

Outrageously popular lasagna in my house.

Makes 8-10 servings

1 pound ground sirloin

1 (14 1/2-ounce) can chopped tomatoes, with juice

1 (4-ounce) can chopped green chilies, drained

2 teaspoons chili powder

1 1/2 teaspoons ground cumin

1 teaspoon minced garlic

Salt and pepper to taste

2 egg whites

2 cups reduced-fat or fat-free cottage cheese

14 (6-inch) corn or flour tortillas, cut into quarters
(corn for Gluten-free option)

1 1/2 cups corn

1 (2 cups) package shredded reduced-fat
Mexican blend cheese

1. Preheat oven 350°F. Coat 13x9x2-inch baking dish with nonstick cooking spray.

2. In large nonstick skillet, cook meat over medium heat until done. Add tomatoes with juice, green chilies, chili powder, cumin, garlic, and season to taste; set aside.

3. In bowl, blend egg whites and cottage cheese well; set aside.

4. Line baking dish with six quartered tortillas. Layer all the corn, half meat mixture, half cheese, four quartered tortillas, then all cottage cheese mixture, remaining half meat mixture, and remaining four quartered tortillas, and top with remaining cheese. Bake, uncovered, 30 minutes.

NUTRIENTS

Calories 239

Protein 25g

Carbohydrate 20g

Fat 7g

Calories from Fat 26%

Saturated Fat 3g

Dietary Fiber 3g

Cholesterol 40mg

Sodium 537mg

Diabetic Exchanges: 3 lean meat, 1 starch, 1 vegetable

I prefer blending the cottage cheese in a food processor until it's smooth. Ricotta cheese may be substituted for the cottage cheese.

STIR-FRY RICE

Turn leftover rice into this scrumptious Asian specialty.

Makes 6 (1-cup) servings

1 tablespoon canola oil

1 cup chopped onion

1/2 cup chopped carrot

1 teaspoon minced garlic

2 egg whites, beaten

3 cups cooked rice (white or brown)

3 tablespoons low-sodium soy sauce

2 teaspoons sesame oil

2 teaspoons finely chopped fresh ginger
  or 1 teaspoon ground ginger

1/2 cup shelled edamame, (if frozen, thaw)

1/2 cup chopped green onion

1 tablespoon sesame seeds, toasted, optional

1. In large nonstick skillet, heat oil and sauté onion, carrot, and garlic 5-7 minutes. Add egg whites stirring, until cooked.

2. Add rice, soy sauce, sesame oil, and ginger cooking and stirring until heated, about 3 minutes. Add edamame and green onion, stirring until well heated. Sprinkle with sesame seeds, if desired.

NUTRIENTS

Calories 184

Calories from Fat 23%

Fat 5g

Saturated Fat 0g

Cholesterol 0mg

Sodium 227mg

Carbohydrates 29g

Dietary Fiber 2g

Total Sugars 4g

Protein 6g

Dietary Exchanges: 1 1/2 starch, 1 vegetable, 1 fat

Be creative and add whatever veggies you have or even leftover seafood, chicken or meat for a heartier version.

Did you know sesame seeds are a great source of calcium?

Toasted sesame seeds may be found in spice section of grocery.

ENERGY BITES

These no-bake bites may be small but they pack a subtlety sweet, yet filling taste of goodness with all my favorite ingredients.

Makes 20-25 balls

1 cup old-fashioned oatmeal

1/3 cup toasted coconut flakes

1/2 cup peanut butter

1/2 cup ground flaxseed

1/2 cup semisweet chocolate chips, optional

1/3 cup honey

1 teaspoon vanilla extract

1. In medium bowl, stir together all ingredients until thoroughly mixed. Let chill in refrigerator 30 minutes.
2. Once chilled, roll into heaping teaspoon-size balls. Store in an airtight container and refrigerate up to 1 week.

 D

NUTRIENTS

Calories 74

Calories from Fat 46%

Fat 4g

Saturated Fat 1g

Cholesterol 0mg

Sodium 28mg

Carbohydrates 8g

Dietary Fiber 1g

Total Sugars 5g

Protein 2g

Dietary Exchanges: 1/2 other carbohydrate, 1 fat

NUTRITIONAL
NUGGET

This perfect combination of complex carbohydrates, healthy fats and protein is a terrific bite to fuel you on the go.

Great Greek Couscous Salad (pg 180)

9

SPICE UP YOUR LIFE

Believe it or not, you have the keys to health right in your pantry – spices! Like fruits and vegetables, spices contain beneficial phytonutrients that can have powerful effects on health. Certain spices seem to have anti–inflammatory effects, and therefore should be considered in arthritis treatment. Always consult a practitioner before starting any herbal treatment.

GARLIC - Garlic has so many health benefits due to its high antioxidant content, such as boosting your immune system, helping to reduce blood pressure as well as reducing the risk for certain cancers. The use of garlic to treat medical ailments dates back to early history. The anti-inflammatory properties of garlic can help to ease arthritic pain and swelling. Garlic contains the mineral selenium, an antioxidant that helps fight free radicals, often responsible for degenerative damage. Rich in sulfur, garlic is also essential in collagen production which is needed in forming cartilage – cushioning joints. Garlic can be eaten throughout the day in raw or cooked form. It is thought to be a very effective home remedy for arthritis.

CURRY/TURMERIC - Turmeric is the key ingredient, an Asian mustard-yellow spice found in curry. Research shows that turmeric may help the body reduce arthritic symptoms. Curcumin is a potent antioxidant found in turmeric with anti-inflammatory properties aiding in reducing pain – fighting free radicals and protecting against cell damage. Consuming moderate amounts of turmeric on a regular basis may help prevent arthritis pain. Turmeric is commonly used in curry dishes.

GINGER - Ginger has been used for centuries because of its medicinal properties. Protecting against cancer, and boosting your immune system, ginger has long been a remedy for nausea and a digestive aid, which is especially important when medicine leaves an upset stomach. This versatile tan root is a potent spice found to have anti-inflammatory compounds that reduce swelling and stiffness. Look for fresh ginger in the produce section of most grocery stores or powdered ginger, found in the spice aisle.

NOTE - Combine turmeric with ginger for added relief of inflammation. Turmeric and ginger are capable of thinning the blood and all spices consumed outside of moderate food preparation and diet should only be used under the supervision of your health practitioner.

Like fruits and vegetables, spices contain beneficial phytonutrients that can have powerful effects on health. Certain spices seem to have anti–inflammatory effects, and therefore should be considered in arthritis treatment.

SNACK MIX

A savory and sweet mix that is hard to beat.

Makes 20 (1/2-cup) servings

3 tablespoons sesame oil

3 tablespoons honey

1 tablespoon low-sodium soy sauce

1 teaspoon garlic powder

4 cups honey-nut toasted rice and honey nut cereal squares

6 cups mini-pretzels

1 cup dry roasted peanuts

1 cup candy-coated chocolate pieces

1. Preheat oven 250°F. Line baking pan with foil.

2. In small bowl, whisk together sesame oil, honey, soy sauce, and garlic powder.

3. On prepared pan, combine cereal squares, pretzels, and peanuts. Add oil mixture and toss with cereal mixture. Bake 25 minutes, stirring once.

4. Turn off oven and remain in oven 1 hour to continue crisping. Cool completely and toss with chocolate candies. Store in an airtight container.

NUTRIENTS

Calories 205

Calories from Fat 36%

Fat 8g

Saturated Fat 2g

Cholesterol 1mg

Sodium 357mg

Carbohydrate 29g

Dietary Fiber 1g

Protein 4g

Diabetic Exchanges: 2 starch, 1 fat

TERRIFIC TIP

Use seasonal chocolate candies for the different holidays.

Leave out the chocolate candies and add dried cranberries, if desired. Or, the mixture can be made without either.

NUTRITIONAL NUGGET

Fortified cereals actually provide a host of nutrients including calcium, iron, fiber, folic acid, and vitamins C, B, and A.

MEATY MEDITERRANEAN PITA NACHOS

D

NUTRIENTS

Calories 209

Calories from Fat 18%

Fat 4g

Saturated Fat 1g

Cholesterol 17mg

Sodium 412mg

Carbohydrates 30g

Dietary Fiber 4g

Total Sugars 3g

Protein 15g

Dietary Exchanges: 2 starch, 1 1/2 lean meat

Greek yogurt is an excellent low fat, low sugar, high protein substitute for plain yogurt or even sour cream.

Buy pita chips (like my sister did) and you don't have to bake pitas.

OMG — Outrageously delicious! My family gave this 5 stars!!

Makes 8 servings

6 whole wheat pitas, split and each half cut into 8 triangles

1/2 pound ground sirloin

1/2 cup chopped onion

1/2 teaspoon minced garlic

1/2 teaspoon ground cumin

Tzatziki sauce, (recipe follows)

1/2 cup chopped red onion

1/2 cup grape tomatoes, sliced in half

1/2 cup chopped peeled cucumber

1/3 cup reduced-fat crumbled feta

3 tablespoons sliced Kalamata olives

1. Preheat oven 400°F. Coat baking pan with nonstick cooking spray.
2. Lay pita triangles on baking pan and bake about 10 minutes or until crispy. Remove from oven.
3. In nonstick skillet, cook meat, onion, and garlic until meat is done. Add cumin; set aside.
4. Arrange crispy pitas on plate. Spread meat over pitas, top with Tzatziki sauce (see recipe) and sprinkle with red onion, tomatoes, cucumber, feta and olives.

TZATZIKI SAUCE

A classic Greek and Turkish creamy sauce that also makes a great dip.

1 cup Greek nonfat plain yogurt

1/2 cup peeled and seeded finely diced cucumber

1 teaspoon minced garlic

1 teaspoon white vinegar

1 tablespoon lemon juice

Salt and pepper to taste

1. In small bowl, combine all ingredients.

Meaty Mediterranean Pita Nachos

GREAT GREEK COUSCOUS SALAD

 D

Quick cooking couscous livens up with these fresh Greek ingredients. Use wild rice for a Gluten-free option.

Makes 8 (1-cup) servings

NUTRIENTS

Calories 219

Calories from Fat 24%

Fat 6g

Saturated Fat 1g

Cholesterol 1mg

Sodium 258mg

Carbohydrates 34g

Dietary Fiber 4g

Total Sugars 2g

Protein 7g

Dietary Exchanges: 2 starch, 1 fat

2 cups water

1/2 teaspoon minced garlic

1 1/3 cups couscous

1/2 cup chopped green onion

2 cups chopped peeled cucumber

3 tablespoons chopped fresh mint leaves or 1 tablespoon dried mint

1 (15-ounce) can cannellini beans, rinsed and drained

1 cup cherry or grape tomato halves

1/3 cup sliced Kalamata olives

1/4 cup lemon juice

2 tablespoons olive oil

1/4 cup crumbled reduced-fat crumbled feta

Salt and pepper to taste

1. In medium pot, bring water and garlic to boil. Add couscous; stir, remove from heat, and cover 7 minutes. Fluff with fork, and transfer to large bowl.
2. Add green onion, cucumber, mint, beans, tomatoes, and olives to couscous, mixing well.
3. In small bowl, mix together lemon juice and olive oil. Toss with couscous, feta and season to taste.

Raid a salad bar in the grocery to make your own portion of Kalamata olives as they really make a difference in this fresh salad.

CHICKEN SALAD WITH ASIAN VINAIGRETTE

Leftover chicken turns into a powerful Asian chicken salad.

Makes 4 (1/2-cup) servings

2 cups cooked skinless, chicken breast chunks

1/3 cup chopped green onion

2 tablespoons chopped parsley

1/4 cup chopped red bell pepper

Vinaigrette (recipe follows)

2 tablespoons sliced almonds, toasted

1. In bowl combine chicken, green onion, parsley, bell pepper. Toss with Vinaigrette (see recipe) and almonds when serving.

ASIAN VINAIGRETTE

2 tablespoons seasoned rice vinegar

1 tablespoon honey

1 tablespoon low-sodium soy sauce

1 tablespoon grated fresh ginger or 1 teaspoon ground ginger

1 teaspoon sesame oil

1 tablespoon olive oil

Dash crushed red pepper flakes

1. In small bowl, whisk together all ingredients.

 D

NUTRIENTS

Calories 210

Calories from Fat 39%

Fat 9g

Saturated Fat 2g

Cholesterol 59mg

Sodium 252mg

Carbohydrates 9g

Dietary Fiber 1g

Total Sugars 8g

Protein 23g

Dietary Exchanges: 1/2 other carbohydrate, 3 lean meat

Known for centuries for its medicinal properties, ginger may help protect against cancer and boost your immune system – also aiding in nausea symptoms.

Serve over mixed greens or stuff in avocado.

THAI COCONUT CURRY CHICKEN

NUTRIENTS

Calories 215

Calories from Fat 41%

Fat 10g

Saturated Fat 2g

Cholesterol 73mg

Sodium 301mg

Carbohydrates 4g

Dietary Fiber 1g

Total Sugars 2g

Protein 27g

Dietary Exchanges: 1/2 other carbohydrate, 3 1/2 lean meat

Add more water to reheat sauce, if necessary.

Peanut sauce is great with chicken or any meat.

Flavorful chicken with a marvelous Peanut Sauce.

Makes 8 servings

1 (14-ounce) can lite coconut milk, reserve 1/2 cup

3 tablespoons Thai red curry paste

2 pounds boneless, skinless thin chicken breasts

Peanut sauce (recipe follows)

1. In resealable plastic bag mix coconut milk and red curry paste. Add chicken and marinate in refrigerator one hour or time permitting.

2. Remove chicken from marinade (discard marinade) and grill or cook in nonstick skillet coated with nonstick cooking spray until golden brown on each side. Serve with Peanut Sauce (see recipe).

PEANUT SAUCE

1 teaspoon canola oil

1 teaspoon red curry paste

1 teaspoon ground turmeric

1/3 cup peanut butter

1/2 cup lite coconut milk (reserved from above)

1/2 cup water

1 teaspoon sugar

1. In small nonstick pot, heat oil and add curry paste and turmeric: stir until fragrant, about 1 minute. Add remaining ingredients and stir until thickened.

CHICKEN CURRY & WHITE BEANS

Curry and turmeric are key to flavor and anti-inflammatory fighters in this fantastic, fast chicken dish with a wonderful sauce. Serve with rice.

 D

Makes 8 (1-cup) servings

2 pounds boneless, skinless chicken tenders

1/4 cup all-purpose flour

1 tablespoon olive oil

1 large onion, chopped

1 teaspoon minced garlic

1 teaspoon ground turmeric

2 tablespoons curry powder

1 (15-ounce) can white beans, rinsed and drained

2 (14-1/2 ounce) cans chopped fire-roasted tomatoes

1 cup Greek nonfat plain yogurt

Salt and pepper to taste

Chopped cilantro, optional garnish

NUTRIENTS

Calories 271

Calories from Fat 17%

Fat 5g

Saturated Fat 1g

Cholesterol 73mg

Sodium 592mg

Carbohydrates 23g

Dietary Fiber 4g

Total Sugars 6g

Protein 32g

Dietary Exchanges: 1 starch, 1 vegetable, 3 1/2 lean meat

1. Coat chicken tenders with flour. In large nonstick skillet, heat oil over medium-high heat. Add chicken and brown on both sides, 3-5 minutes. Add onion, cooking until tender, stirring.

2. Add garlic, turmeric, curry powder and cook, stirring, 1 minute. Add white beans and tomatoes. Reduce heat and cook, covered 15-20 minutes or until chicken is tender.

3. Remove from heat. Stir in yogurt. Season to taste. Sprinkle with cilantro, if desired.

NUTRITIONAL
NUGGET

Turmeric gives curry its deep yellow color, and research has shown the spice to have potent antioxidant, anti-inflammatory benefits.

GLAZED GINGER CHICKEN

Bold flavors give this simple chicken dish lots of pizazz.

Makes 8 servings

NUTRIENTS

Calories 152

Calories from Fat 25%

Fat 4g

Saturated Fat 1g

Cholesterol 73mg

Sodium 204mg

Carbohydrates 3g

Dietary Fiber 0g

Total Sugars 2g

Protein 24g

Dietary Exchanges: 3 lean meat

2 teaspoons ground ginger

4 tablespoons Hoisin sauce

2 teaspoons low-sodium soy sauce

2 teaspoons olive oil

2 pounds boneless skinless chicken breast tenders (or thighs)

1. In resealable plastic bag, mix ginger, hoisin sauce, soy sauce and olive oil. Add chicken. Marinate one hour or time permitting.

2. To grill: place chicken (discard marinade) on preheated grill at low to medium. Grill each side 4-6 minutes. Remove from grill and let sit 5 minutes. If desired, broil in oven on foil lined pan.

Known for its anti-nausea affects, try this simple ginger-rich meal when you may not be feeling well.

CHICKEN CURRY WITH SPINACH & TOMATOES

A simple combination of curry, coconut milk and tomato packs tremendous flavor into this sensational chicken dish. Serve over rice.

Makes 8 servings

2 pounds boneless, skinless chicken breasts

2 teaspoons curry powder

Salt and pepper to taste

1/2 cup chopped onion

1 teaspoon minced garlic

1 (14-ounce) can lite coconut milk

1 (14 1/2-ounce) can diced tomatoes, drained

3 cups packed baby spinach

1. Season chicken with curry and with salt and pepper.

2. In large nonstick pan coated with nonstick cooking spray, brown chicken breasts on both sides, 5-7 minutes. Add onion and garlic, and continue sautéing 5 minutes, stirring.

3. Add coconut milk and tomatoes, bring to boil, reduce heat and cook about 15-20 minutes or until chicken is tender. Add spinach, and cook until wilted, about 2 minutes.

NUTRIENTS

Calories 178

Calories from Fat 29%

Fat 6g

Saturated Fat 2g

Cholesterol 73mg

Sodium 241mg

Carbohydrates 6g

Dietary Fiber 1g

Total Sugars 3g

Protein 25g

Dietary Exchanges: 1 vegetable, 3 lean meat

You know spinach is loaded with healthy nutrients by the rich color green; boasting powerful antioxidant protection — add it to any dish you can — even smoothies!

I like to use fire-roasted tomatoes for a richer flavor.

KOREAN BEEF TACOS

Take a taco detour with these unbelievably tasty tacos.

Makes 6 beef tacos

2 tablespoons sesame oil, divided

1 tablespoon minced ginger or 1 teaspoon ground ginger

1 tablespoon lemon juice

3 tablespoons low-sodium soy sauce

1 tablespoon honey

1 teaspoon minced garlic

1 green onion, chopped

1 1/2 pounds flank or skirt steak

6 corn taco shells

2 tomatoes, chopped

Sesame Dressing (recipe follows)

1. In large resealable plastic bag, mix 1 tablespoon sesame oil, ginger, lemon juice, soy sauce, honey, garlic, and green onion. Add meat and marinate in refrigerator as time permits.

2. In large nonstick skillet, heat remaining 1 tablespoon sesame oil, and add beef; cooking 2-3 minutes on each side or until medium rare (can broil, if prefer). Slice meat and fill tacos with meat, tomatoes and top with Sesame Dressing (see recipe).

SESAME DRESSING

1 tablespoon minced ginger or 1 teaspoon ground ginger

3 tablespoons lemon juice

4 tablespoons low-sodium soy sauce

2 teaspoons sesame seeds, toasted

1 green onion, chopped

1. In small bowl, mix all ingredients.

NUTRIENTS

Calories 306

Calories from Fat 43%

Fat 15g

Saturated Fat 4g

Cholesterol 65mg

Sodium 595mg

Carbohydrates 18g

Dietary Fiber 2g

Total Sugars 7g

Protein 25g

Dietary Exchanges: 1 starch, 3 lean meat, 1 fat

TERRIFIC TIP

The meat marinade may be used for any meat to grill.

When slicing flank steak: let sit 5 minutes and slice against grain.

NUTRITIONAL NUGGET

Just a quarter cup of sesame seeds provide more calcium than an entire cup of milk.

Look for toasted sesame seeds in Asian section.

INDONESIAN BEEF WITH COCONUT RICE

The spice and seasonings make this an out-of-this world recipe. Serve with the melt-in-your-mouth coconut rice that perfectly contrasts the beef.

Makes 6 (1/2-cup) beef servings

1 1/2 pounds sirloin, trimmed and thinly sliced

1 red bell pepper, cored and sliced

2 tablespoons minced fresh ginger

1 teaspoon minced garlic

1 teaspoon ground cumin

1/2 teaspoon ground cloves

1 1/3 cups low-sodium fat-free beef broth

Salt and pepper

1/2 cup chopped green onion

Coconut Rice (recipe follows)

1. In large nonstick skillet coated with nonstick cooking spray, cook meat over medium-high heat 5 minutes.
2. Add red pepper, ginger, garlic, cumin, cloves and broth. Bring to boil, reduce heat, and simmer until meat is tender, about 10 minutes. Season to taste and sprinkle with green onion. Serve with Coconut Rice (see recipe).

COCONUT RICE

If you don't have basmati rice, you may use any rice.

1 1/4 cups water

1 cup lite coconut milk

1 cup basmati rice

1. In pot, bring water and coconut milk to boil. Add rice, reduce heat, cover, and cook until liquid is absorbed and rice is tender, about 20 minutes.

NUTRIENTS

Calories 291

Calories from Fat 24%

Fat 8g

Saturated Fat 3g

Cholesterol 65mg

Sodium 175mg

Carbohydrates 27g

Dietary Fiber 2g

Total Sugars 2g

Protein 28g

Dietary Exchanges: 2 starch, 3 lean meat

You can use lean top round (a less expensive cut) but cook longer.

Ground ginger may be substituted using 2 teaspoons.

Give fresh ginger a try — it's easy to peel and grate.

Red Velvet Berry Trifle (pg 199)

BECAUSE I HAVE *a* SWEET TOOTH

Chocolate covered strawberries - since strawberries are a healthy fruit and chocolate contains nutritious antioxidants– they must be considered a health food! Desserts and sweets are often considered bad for us that should be removed from a healthy diet. However, another way to look at sweet treats are how they can add nutrition that is actually good for us so as not to always have to stay away from the dessert table. Although moderation is still important, consider dessert a vehicle to getting more healthy fruits, nuts and dairy in your diet. This chapter includes sweet treats that have been trimmed up while still tasting as terrific as ever – you will never miss the full fat and sugar. It is unrealistic to think that you will never eat sweets again, but with these tips and recipes you can stay on track to maintain your overall health and weight control.

When eating dessert always pair it with a fruit or berries to make sure you are getting in your daily servings.

- Whether you choose strawberries, blueberries, raspberries, cranberries, or blackberries, these little jewels are packed with fiber and antioxidants that help slow the aging process from the inside out.

- Berries deliver delicious taste and nutrition with few calories. Frozen do the trick as well as fresh, and can be in the freezer year-round.

- Nuts are often included in desserts such as cakes, cookies and brownies. Nuts tend to be higher in fat and calories so don't go "nuts" eating too many, however they do contain a host of health benefits making them worthy of being included in your meals and snacks.

- Nuts provide fiber, protein, potassium, magnesium, omega-3 fatty acids and vitamins E and B6 – making them a great addition to reduce inflammation.

- Did you know that pecans contain the highest amount of antioxidants than any other nut?

Dairy products are good sources of protein, vitamin D, potassium, and especially calcium, which is very important for bone and muscle mass.

- You don't have to just drink your milk; foods can include other sources of calcium such as low-fat yogurt, cheese and cottage cheese are great for you too!

- Calcium is absorbed best from foods rather than supplements- make sure to get at least three servings of calcium-rich foods every day.

- Dairy is important for building strong teeth and bones, but can also help in weight management.

This chapter includes sweet treats that have been trimmed up while still tasting as terrific as ever – you will never miss the full fat and sugar.

APPLE BREAD

An apple a day keeps the doc away; another reason to enjoy this delightfully delicious quick bread.

Makes 16 slices

1/3 cup canola oil

3/4 cup sugar

2 eggs

1/3 cup buttermilk

1 teaspoon vanilla extract

2 cups all-purpose flour

1 teaspoon ground cinnamon

1 teaspoon baking soda

2 cups peeled and diced baking apples

1. Preheat oven 350°F. Coat 9x5x3-inch loaf pan with nonstick cooking spray.

2. In bowl, mix together oil and sugar until light. Add eggs, one at a time, beating well. Add buttermilk and vanilla.

3. In another bowl, combine flour, cinnamon, and baking soda. Add to sugar mixture, stirring just until combined. Stir in diced apples. Transfer batter into prepared pan.

4. Bake 45-50 minutes or until toothpick inserted comes out clean.

   D

NUTRIENTS

Calories 156

Calories from Fat 32%

Fat 6g

Saturated Fat 1g

Cholesterol 23mg

Sodium 94mg

Carbohydrates 24g

Dietary Fiber 1g

Total Sugars 11g

Protein 3g

Dietary Exchanges: 1 1/2 starch, 1 fat

NUTRITIONAL **NUGGET**

Eating an apple a day — you will get a good dose of the fiber, pectin, helping you control appetite, maintain a healthy weight and regulate your digestive system.

TERRIFIC TIP

Sprinkle 1 teaspoon cinnamon over ground coffee before brewing — process of brewing coffee is one of the best ways to get good stuff out of the spice.

BANANA CHOCOLATE CHIP BREAD

What can be better than a rich chocolate banana bread with chocolate chips — need I say more?

Makes 16 slices

1/4 cup canola oil

1/2 cup light brown sugar

1/4 cup sugar

1 teaspoon vanilla extract

2 eggs

1 1/2 cups mashed bananas (3-4 ripe bananas)

1 1/2 cups all-purpose flour

1/4 cup cocoa

1 teaspoon baking soda

1 teaspoon baking powder

1/4 cup skim milk

1/2 cup dark or semisweet chocolate chips

1/2 cup chopped pecans

1. Preheat oven 350°F. Coat 9x5x3-inch loaf pan with nonstick cooking spray.

2. In mixing bowl, beat oil, brown sugar, sugar and vanilla until creamy. Add eggs, mixing well. Add bananas.

3. In small bowl, combine flour, cocoa, baking soda and baking powder. Stir in flour mixture and milk; mixing only until combined. Stir in chocolate chips and pecans. Transfer batter into prepared pan.

4. Bake 45-50 minutes, or until a toothpick inserted in the center comes out almost clean.

NUTRIENTS

Calories 206

Calories from Fat 37%

Fat 9g

Saturated Fat 2g

Cholesterol 23mg

Sodium 117mg

Carbohydrates 30g

Dietary Fiber 2g

Total Sugars 17g

Protein 3g

Dietary Exchanges: 2 other carbohydrate, 2 fat

NUTRITIONAL NUGGET

A prime food for arthritis sufferers, bananas offer loads of important nutrients to help build collagen and beat inflammation such as vitamin C, B-6 and folate.

TERRIFIC TIP

Don't overcook: Chocolate cooks after removed from oven.

CHOCOLATE ZUCCHINI MUFFINS

A morsel of chocolate pops out in this rich chocolaty muffin.

Makes 18 muffins

2 eggs
1/3 cup Greek nonfat plain yogurt
1/3 cup canola oil
3/4 cup sugar
1 teaspoon vanilla extract
1 1/2 cups all-purpose flour
1/3 cup cocoa
1/2 teaspoon ground cinnamon
1 teaspoon baking soda
1 1/2 cups shredded zucchini (about 2 medium zucchini)
1/2 cup semisweet or dark chocolate chips
1/2 cup coarsely chopped walnuts, optional

1. Preheat oven 350°F. Line muffin tins with paper liners.
2. In mixing bowl, beat eggs until foamy. Add yogurt, oil, sugar, and vanilla; beating until creamy.
3. In small bowl, combine flour, cocoa, cinnamon, and baking soda. Add flour mixture to sugar mixture, stirring only until combined.
4. Add zucchini, chocolate chips, and walnuts, if desired, stirring only until just combined. Fill prepared muffin tins. Bake 17-20 minutes. Don't over bake.

NUTRIENTS

Calories 158
Calories from Fat 38%
Fat 7g
Saturated Fat 2g
Cholesterol 21mg
Sodium 80mg
Carbohydrates 22g
Dietary Fiber 1g
Total Sugars 12g
Protein 3g
Dietary Exchanges: 1 1/2 other carbohydrate, 1 1/2 fat

TERRIFIC TIP

Keep in freezer to pull out for snacks.

Unsweetened cocoa is a superstar source of flavonoids.

NUTRITIONAL NUGGET

By adding zucchini to your sweet treats, you are adding an excellent source of the powerful antioxidant Vitamin A.

OATMEAL NUT COOKIES

   D

Back to basics with this yummy, crispy oatmeal cookie.

Makes 48 cookies

NUTRIENTS

Calories 78

Calories from Fat 47%

Fat 4g

Saturated Fat 1g

Cholesterol 6mg

Sodium 37mg

Carbohydrates 9g

Dietary Fiber 1g

Total Sugars 5g

Protein 1g

Dietary Exchanges: 1/2
other carbohydrate, 1 fat

4 tablespoons butter

1/4 cup canola oil

1/2 cup sugar

1/2 cup light brown sugar

2 teaspoons vanilla extract

1 egg

1 1/4 cups all-purpose flour

1 teaspoon baking soda

1 teaspoon ground cinnamon

2 cups old-fashioned oatmeal

1 cup chopped nuts (pecans or walnuts)

1. Preheat oven 375°F. Coat baking pan with nonstick cooking spray.

2. In mixing bowl, beat butter, oil, sugar, brown sugar, and vanilla until creamy. Add egg, beat well.

3. In another bowl, combine flour, baking soda and cinnamon. Gradually add flour mixture to sugar mixture, mixing just until combined. Stir in oatmeal and nuts.

4. Drop dough by teaspoonfuls onto prepared baking pan. Bake 8-10 minutes, or until cookies are lightly browned on bottom.

*Use ergonomic utensils
with rubber grips for
ease on joints.*

*Did you know that pecans
are higher in antioxidants
than any other nut?*

YAM CHOCOLATE SPICE BARS

One bite of this incredible fall favorite made with a spice cake mix, yam filling and chocolate chips was a taste sensation. Everyone requested this recipe. Good use for leftover cooked sweet potatoes.

Makes 48 squares

1 (18.25-ounce) box spice cake mix

1/2 cup butter, melted

1 egg

1 (8-ounce) package reduced-fat cream cheese

1 (15-ounce) can sweet potatoes, drained and mashed

1 (16-ounce) box confectioners' sugar

2 egg whites

1 teaspoon vanilla extract

2/3 cup semisweet chocolate chips

1. Preheat oven to 350° F. Coat 13x9x2-inch baking pan with nonstick cooking spray.

2. In mixing bowl, beat together cake mix, butter, and egg until well mixed. Spread batter into prepared pan.

3. In mixing bowl, beat together cream cheese, sweet potatoes, confectioners' sugar, egg whites, and vanilla until creamy. Stir in chocolate chips. Pour mixture over batter in pan.

4. Bake 40-50 minutes or until top is golden brown. Cool to room temperature and cut into squares.

NUTRIENTS

Calories 134

Calories from Fat 31%

Fat 5g

Saturated Fat 3g

Cholesterol 12mg

Sodium 116mg

Carbohydrates 22g

Dietary Fiber 0g

Total Sugars 16g

Protein 2g

Dietary Exchanges: 1 1/2 other carbohydrate, 1 fat

TERRIFIC TIP

Most bar cookies freeze well, so feel free to make ahead and pull out when you have a craving.

NUTRITIONAL NUGGET

You know yams are an excellent source of antioxidant-rich carotenoids because of their deep orange color — great for reducing inflammation.

FRESH FIG BUNDT CAKE

   D

You'll become a fig fan after one bite of this fabulous cake.

Makes 20 servings

NUTRIENTS

Calories 194

Calories from Fat 32%

Fat 7g

Saturated Fat 1g

Cholesterol 21g

Sodium 11mg

Carbohydrates 30g

Dietary Fiber 1g

Total Sugars 20g

Protein 3g

Diabetic Exchanges: 2 other carbohydrate, 1 1/2 fat

Fresh dates may be used for figs. If using dried figs, it might not be quite as moist, but I am sure as good.

1/3 cup canola oil

1 1/2 cups sugar

1 teaspoon vanilla extract

2 eggs

1 egg white

2 cups all-purpose flour

1 teaspoon baking soda

1 1/2 teaspoons ground cinnamon

1 cup buttermilk

1 cup coarsely chopped fresh figs, stems removed

1/2 cup chopped pecans

Glaze (recipe follows)

1. Preheat oven 350°F. Coat Bundt pan with nonstick cooking spray.
2. In mixing bowl, cream oil, sugar, and vanilla. Add eggs and egg white, one at a time, beating well after each addition.
3. In small bowl, combine flour, baking soda, and cinnamon. Add flour mixture to sugar mixture, alternating with buttermilk and ending with flour, beating after each addition.
4. Stir in figs and pecans. Bake 40-45 minutes, until top springs back when touched. Let cake cool 10 minutes, then invert onto serving plate. Pour Glaze (see recipe) over hot cake.

GLAZE

1/4 cup sugar

2 teaspoons light corn syrup

1 tablespoon butter

1/4 cup buttermilk

1/4 teaspoon baking soda

1/2 teaspoon vanilla extract

1. In small nonstick pot, combine all ingredients except vanilla and bring to boil 4 minutes over medium heat, stirring constantly. Add vanilla and pour over hot cake.

Fresh Fig Bundt Cake

Oatmeal Cake with Coconut Pecan Topping

OATMEAL CAKE WITH COCONUT PECAN TOPPING

NUTRIENTS

Calories 154

Calories from Fat 44%

Fat 8g

Saturated Fat 2g

Cholesterol 14mg

Sodium 60mg

Carbohydrates 20g

Dietary Fiber 1g

Total Sugars 13g

Protein 2g

Dietary Exchanges: 1 1/2
other carbohydrate,
1 1/2 fat

NUTRITIONAL
NUGGET

*1 teaspoon cinnamon has
more antioxidants than
1/2 cup blueberries.*

*Dust 1/2 teaspoon
cinnamon on apple slices
and place in container for
later — spice prevents fruit
from browning.*

Incredibly moist cake with a more incredible topping.

Makes 16 servings

1/2 cup old-fashioned oatmeal

3/4 cup boiling water

1/3 cup sugar

1/3 cup light brown sugar

3/4 cup all-purpose flour

1 teaspoon ground cinnamon

1/2 teaspoon baking soda

1 egg

1/4 cup canola oil

Coconut Pecan Topping (recipe follows)

1. Preheat oven 350°F. Coat 9x9x2-inch pan with nonstick spray. In bowl, combine oatmeal and boiling water; let stand 5 minutes. Stir in remaining ingredients. Transfer to prepared pan. Bake 13-15 minutes or until almost done.

2. Turn oven to broil. Carefully spread Coconut Pecan Topping (see recipe) over top of cake and broil about 3 minutes or until topping is bubbly and just brown (watch carefully).

COCONUT PECAN TOPPING

1 tablespoon butter, melted

1/4 cup light brown sugar

1/3 cup flaked coconut

1/2 cup chopped pecans

1/4 cup skim milk

1. In small bowl combine all ingredients.

See page 197 for photo

RED VELVET BERRY TRIFLE

A few mixes and boxes come together for this stupendous trifle, layering red velvet cake, heavenly pudding, berries and whipped topping.

Makes 25 servings

1 (18.25-ounce) box Red Velvet cake mix

1/4 cup canola oil

2 eggs

1 1/3 cups water

3 ounces reduced-fat cream cheese

3 cups skim milk, divided

2 (4-serving) boxes instant white chocolate pudding and pie filling

1/4 cup orange juice

3 cups sliced strawberries, raspberries, blueberries or combination

1 (8-ounce) container frozen nonfat whipped topping, thawed

1. Preheat oven 350°F. Coat two (9-inch) round cake pans with nonstick cooking spray.

2. In mixing bowl, combine cake mix, oil, eggs, and water, blending until well mixed. Pour batter into prepared pans and bake 20 minutes or until toothpick inserted comes out clean.

3. Meanwhile, in bowl mix together cream cheese and a little milk to blend. Add remaining milk and both boxes of pudding, mixing and following directions on box.

4. In trifle bowl or large glass bowl, layer cake, drizzle with 2 tablespoons orange juice, half the pudding, berries, and whipped topping. Repeat layers ending with whipped topping.

NUTRIENTS

Calories 182

Calories from Fat 28%

Fat 6g

Saturated Fat 2g

Cholesterol 18mg

Sodium 275mg

Carbohydrates 30g

Dietary Fiber 1g

Total Sugars 19g

Protein 3g

Dietary Exchanges: 2 other carbohydrate, 1 fat

NUTRITIONAL **NUGGET**

You might as well get a bite of nutritious berries with your luscious dessert — leaving you with an extra dose of vitamin C in your sweet treat.

TERRIFIC TIP

Dark chocolate pairs with berries — both packed with inflammation soothing antioxidants.

BERRY PARFAIT

 D

Light and delightful, strawberries or your favorite berries layered with a luscious cream cheese layer and ladyfingers.

Makes 16 (1/2-cup) servings

2/3 cup seedless sugar-free raspberry preserves

1/4 cup orange juice

6 ounces reduced-fat cream cheese

1/4 cup sugar

1 teaspoon vanilla extract

1 (8-ounce) container frozen nonfat whipped topping, thawed, divided

2 (3-ounce) packages ladyfingers, split in half (24)

1 1/2 cups strawberries, stemmed and sliced

1. In small bowl, mix together preserves and orange juice.
2. In mixing bowl, cream together cream cheese, sugar, and vanilla until light. Mix in whipped topping reserving, 1/2 cup for topping.
3. Line bottom of an oblong small dish with split ladyfingers. Layer with preserves mixture, cream cheese layer, and top with strawberries. Repeat layers with remaining ladyfingers, preserves and cream cheese layer.
4. Carefully top with thin layer of remaining whipped topping. Top with remaining strawberries. Refrigerate.

NUTRIENTS

Calories 128

Calories from fat 24%

Fat 3g

Saturated Fat 1g

Cholesterol 9mg

Sodium 79mg

Carbohydrate 23g

Dietary Fiber 1g

Sugars 11g

Protein 2g

Diabetic Exchanges: 1 1/2 carbohydrate, 1/2 fat

Use raspberries so you don't have to even cut the strawberries. This recipe works well in individual servings.

Angel food cake may be substituted for Lady Fingers.

You will hardly believe this luscious treat is diabetic-friendly so there is always room for dessert!

OATMEAL PECAN PIE

Pecan pie and oatmeal partner together for a melt-in-your-mouth divine dessert. Turn into a chocolate pie by adding about 1/3 cup dark chocolate chips.

Makes 8-10 servings

1/2 cup light brown sugar

1/2 cup light corn syrup

2 eggs

2 teaspoons vanilla extract

2/3 cup old-fashioned oatmeal

3/4 cup coarsely chopped pecans, toasted

1 (9-inch) unbaked pie shell

1. Preheat oven 325°F.
2. In bowl, whisk together brown sugar, corn syrup, eggs, and vanilla.
3. Stir in oatmeal and pecans. Pour into pie shell. Bake 40-45 minutes or until center is set. Cool completely.

NUTRIENTS

Calories 272

Calories from Fat 40%

Fat 13g

Saturated Fat 3g

Cholesterol 40mg

Sodium 139mg

Carbohydrates 39g

Dietary Fiber 1g

Total Sugars 16g

Protein 3g

Dietary Exchanges: 2 1/2 other carbohydrate, 3 fat

If using refrigerated pie crust, coat the pie plate with nonstick cooking spray first to easily remove pie.

PEACH CRISP

Use fresh or frozen peaches for this luscious cobbler with an oatmeal crumbly topping.

Makes 6 (1/2-cup) servings

1 (16-ounce) package frozen peaches, thawed
1 tablespoon cornstarch
2 tablespoons sugar
1 tablespoon lemon juice
2 tablespoons butter
2 tablespoons light brown sugar
1 teaspoon vanilla extract
1/3 cup all-purpose flour
1/2 teaspoon ground cinnamon
1/8 teaspoon baking soda
3/4 cup old-fashioned oatmeal

1. Preheat oven 350ºF.
2. Lay fruit in oblong 2-quart baking dish.
3. In small bowl, mix cornstarch and sugar. Toss cornstarch mixture and lemon juice with peaches in baking dish.
4. In medium bowl, mix together butter, brown sugar, and vanilla. In small bowl, stir together flour, cinnamon and baking soda, and mix with oatmeal and butter mixture until crumbly. Sprinkle on top peaches.
5. Bake 45 minutes, or until topping is brown and bubbly.

NUTRIENTS

Calories 172
Calories from fat 26%
Fat 5g
Saturated Fat 3g
Cholesterol 10mg
Sodium 62mg
Carbohydrate 29g
Dietary Fiber 3g
Sugar 12g
Protein 3g
Dietary Exchanges: 2 other carbohydrate, 1 fat

TERRIFIC TIP

Any fruit, fresh or frozen, may be substituted for peaches.

NUTRITIONAL NUGGET

The yellow-orange color of peaches lets you know they are rich in beta-carotene, protecting the body against free radicals which contributes to joint damage.

NO BAKE COOKIES

An easy quick sweet fix and best of all, these ingredients are probably already in your pantry.

Makes 48 cookies

1/2 cup graham cracker crumbs
3 cups old-fashioned oatmeal
1 cup sugar
1/3 cup cocoa
1/2 cup skim milk
1/2 cup butter
1/2 cup peanut butter
1 teaspoon vanilla extract

1. In medium bowl, combine graham cracker crumbs and oatmeal; set aside.
2. In large nonstick pot, heat sugar, cocoa, milk, and butter, stirring until dissolved. Bring mixture to boil, and boil 2 minutes (not less).
3. Remove from heat. Stir in peanut butter and vanilla until well combined. Quickly add oatmeal mixture and beat by hand until thickened (a few minutes), if necessary.
4. Drop by teaspoonfuls onto waxed paper. Refrigerate until firm, and store in the refrigerator or cool place.

NUTRIENTS

Calories 75
Calories from Fat 44%
Fat 4g
Saturated Fat 2g
Cholesterol 5mg
Sodium 35mg
Carbohydrates 9g
Dietary Fiber 1g
Total Sugars 5g
Protein 2g
Dietary Exchanges:
1/2 other carbohydrate,
1 fat

Oatmeal is an excellent source of fiber, vitamins and minerals.

Be sure to use light weight ergonomic cooking utensils for easier grips and non-slip handles.

INDEX